Gardeners' World magazine

201 Ideas for growing fruit and veg

Gardeners' World magazine

201 Ideas for growing fruit and veg

BBC BOOKS

10 9 8 7 6 5 4 3 2 1

Published in 2011 by BBC Books, an imprint of Ebury Publishing.
A Random House Group Company
Text © *Gardeners' World Magazine*
Photographs © *Gardeners' World Magazine*
Book design © Woodlands Books Ltd 2011

The Random House Group Limited Reg. No. 954009

Addresses for companies within the Random House Group
can be found at www.randomhouse.co.uk

A CIP catalogue record for this book is available from the
British Library.

The Random House Group Limited supports the Forest
Stewardship Council (FSC), the leading international forest
certification organisation. All our titles that are printed on
Greenpeace approved FSC certified paper carry the FSC logo.
Our paper procurement policy can be found at
www.rbooks.co.uk/environment

Mixed Sources
Product group from well-managed
forests and other controlled sources
www.fsc.org Cert no. SGS-COC-005091
© 1996 Forest Stewardship Council
FSC

Project editor: Laura Higginson
Designer: Kathryn Gammon

Colour origination by: Dot Gradations Ltd, UK
Printed and bound in UK by Butler, Tanner and Dennis

To buy books by your favourite authors and register for offers,
visit www.rbooks.co.uk

Contents

Introduction

Growing your own, and then eating the herbs, vegetables and fruits of your labour, is incredibly satisfying. It's a great way to save money and keep yourself healthy, as you know exactly how the food you are eating has been grown. You're also doing your bit to help the environment by cutting down on food miles to your plate.

Having access to an allotment is one of the best ways in which you can give your crops the space to flourish. But don't worry if you're one of the many held on a waiting list, or feel you can't commit to such a big plot; the good news is that lack of space won't prevent you discovering the joys of growing your own food – because even the smallest spaces can be productive. Whether you've got a tiny front or back garden, or even just a balcony, you can still grow a wide range of produce. The key is choosing the right varieties of seeds and plants to suit your soil and space.

To help make growing your own easier, here at *Gardeners' World Magazine* we've collected together our top ideas into one book. You'll find suggestions to suit all sizes and shapes of gardens, starting with a whole chapter on containers for gardeners with only a window ledge to spare. Try growing beetroot and carrots in pots *(page 29)* or herbs in hanging baskets *(page 22)*.

For those of you with gravel rather than grass, try growing thyme between the stones *(page 38)*. If you have wall space to use, grow plants upwards, such as wild strawberries in wall pots *(page 28)*, and don't be put off if your garden doesn't get much sunshine – you can still grow raspberries in shady corners *(page 78)*.

As well as advice on the best times of year to plant and harvest your crops, you'll find tips on planning your space *(page 36)* and improving your soil *(page 41)*, how to make your own compost to feed your garden *(page 57)* and how to ward off pests and diseases. This book has all the inspiration and tips you need for making the most of your outside space – so the sooner you get growing, the sooner you'll be eating!

Cabbages in crates, page 18

Containers

Unusual containers

Have fun growing crops in unusual pots.

Time to plant: spring–summer

You don't have to stick to conventional pots to grow vegetables – anything will do, as long as it has adequate drainage holes and enough room for the crop to develop properly.

Old fruit crates, olive-oil tins and metal troughs make fun containers that are large enough for crops such as baby beetroots and turnips, salad leaves, and all sorts of herbs. Or, as here, develop a kitchen theme with edible pot-marigold flowers and salad leaves bursting out of an old bread bin, or a colander of radishes.

Make sure the container drains properly by drilling a few holes in the base, if there aren't any, and adding a layer of crocks over the bottom before putting in the compost. Some containers may be too well drained, such as crates and colanders, in which case you need to line them with perforated polythene in the same way as you would a hanging basket.

TIP Use a multi-purpose compost rather than garden soil, which can contain weed seeds.

Super scents

Every time you brush past this pot, this highly aromatic collection of herbs will release their delicious perfumes.

Time to plant: spring

Most herbs originate in hot, dry climates and dislike British cold, wet winters. So growing such herbs in pots is the perfect solution, as they can easily be brought indoors for the winter.

Serrated-leaved *Lavandula* x *christiana* makes an attractive alternative to ordinary lavender. It's on the tender side, but if you bring it indoors when the weather turns cold it will get it through the winter unscathed. Woolly thyme (*Thymus pseudolanuginosus*) also benefits from winter protection as it hates wet ground. This thyme has wonderful tactile leaves, which are topped by pretty pinky-mauve flowers, which cover the plant all summer.

Many herbs have colourful foliage, and sages offer some of the widest range of varieties. In this pot we've used golden-leaved sage (*Salvia officinalis* 'Icterina'), but you'll also find purple and tricolour types on offer. All sages produce purple-blue flowers in summer and are delicious in cooking.

A prostrate rosemary placed at the front of this pot helps soften its edges. There are a number of varieties that have this unusual habit, such as *Rosmarinus officinalis* Prostratus Group, and they make a useful alternative to the more commonly seen upright sorts. They're just as tasty in cooking and are covered in flowers from spring onwards.

TIP Herbs love sunshine, so put them in the sunniest place you can. A south-facing spot is ideal as they can bake in the sun all day.

Unusual containers

Super scents

Tomatoes in pots

Growing tomatoes in pots is easy, if you keep them well watered and fed.

Time to plant: spring–early summer

There are hundreds of varieties of tomatoes available, and many have been developed specially for container culture. Although you can sow seeds early in the year, it's often simpler to buy ready-grown tomato plants from a nursery or garden centre – especially if you only need a few plants. You can plant these outdoors in late spring or early summer, once the risk of frost has passed.

Choose a large pot with plenty of room for the roots to grow, as tomatoes are vigorous, and place in a sunny, warm spot. Water regularly, probably daily in hot weather, adding a high-potash tomato feed every week in summer. Watering is the tricky thing to get right with tomatoes: too much and the flavour is spoiled, too little and the fruit becomes marked or the skins split. Sinking a finger into the compost to judge its moisture content will help. If in doubt, little and often is better than no water, followed by a good soaking.

Good varieties include 'Totem', a compact bush plant that's perfect for smaller containers; 'Gardener's Delight', a cordon type; 'Balconi Yellow', which has small yellow fruits.

TIP Go for one of the bush types rather than a cordon variety, as they're far easier to grow and look much better in pots.

Standard currant

Potted black-, red- and whitecurrants are fruitful and easy to manage in a small space.

Time to plant: spring–early summer

Trained standard plants are ideal for small gardens as they grow well in containers. Red- and whitecurrants are easy to train in shapes like cordons and fans to make the most of a small space. Prune red- and whitecurrants in winter, and blackcurrants after fruiting.

One plant can produce a substantial quantity of fruit, providing it's kept well watered while the fruits are developing. Grow them in a large container or pot in a fertile, rich soil with plenty of garden compost mixed in, and protect the developing fruit from birds with netting.

Good varieties for pots include blackcurrant 'Ben Sarek', which is hardy and has a good flavour; redcurrant 'Red Lake', which produces masses of jewel-like fruits; 'White Versailles', a classic whitecurrant variety.

TIP Currants prefer cooler conditions and are happy to grow in some shade.

Standard currant

Tomatoes in containers

Magic carpet

Recycled containers add an individual touch to your displays. The only limit to what you can use is your imagination.

Time to plant: spring

Indulge in a scented carpet of colourful leaves with this display of different types of thyme. Most garden centres will have a reasonable selection of varieties on offer, but to get the widest choice, buy your plants from a specialist herb nursery.

This display uses no less than six varieties of thyme: broad-leaved (*Thymus pulegioides*), lemon-scented (*T.* x *citriodorus*), golden (*T. pulegioides* 'Aureus'), variegated (*T. citriodorus* 'Golden Queen'), silvery (*T. vulgaris* 'Silver Posie'), and common thyme (*T. vulgaris*). All these herbs enjoy a sunny spot and well-drained compost – use a loam-based John Innes compost with extra grit added to improve the drainage.

As an evergreen herb, thyme can be picked for the kitchen at any time of year, and any leaves you can't use straight away can be dried for use later on. They don't need much maintenance either. Just give the plants a quick trim if they start to become unruly.

TIP Make sure your container drains freely by filling the base with gravel or broken-up chunks from polystyrene trays before adding compost.

A taste of the Orient

It's surprising how many oriental vegetables and herbs can be grown successfully in Britain. This group of containers features some of the most popular types.

Time to plant: late spring–mid-summer

Lemon grass forms a big, impressive plant once it gets going, and is the centrepiece of our group. Its stems have an intense lemon-like flavour that's delicious in Thai cookery. The plant can be harvested all summer long, then when autumn arrives it should be left to go dormant, then brought into a frost-free place over winter.

Thai basil has a different flavour to the Italian types of this popular herb. It's a favourite ingredient in Thai and Vietnamese cooking. Plants are easy to raise from seed each spring.

The final two pots contain pak choi and mixed oriental salad leaves. You'll find a good selection of seeds available in mail-order seed catalogues. Their only peculiarity is that they shouldn't be sown until after midsummer in the UK. This is because they have a tendency to produce flowers instead of leaves if sown when the days are lengthening. Wait until midsummer – when the days start to shorten again – and you won't have any problems.

TIP Planting in separate pots means you can get ahead on the lemon grass and Thai basil to get the most from them over the summer. Then you can add the pak choi and oriental salad leaves to the display at their optimum planting time.

Magic carpet

A taste of the Orient

Salsa!

If you're a fan of Mexican food, this colourful collection of pots is perfect for you. It contains everything you need to make your own salsa.

Time to plant: mid- to late spring

Chillies are best grown in pots so they can be easily moved indoors when the weather cools. Larger-fruited varieties are great to flavour stuffing as well as salsa. The keys to success with chillies are to feed once a week with tomato food as soon as the first fruits appear and to keep the compost moist – dry conditions will cause the flower buds to drop.

Tomatoes also do well in containers, as long as they're big enough. Large-fruited tomato varieties ripen best in the greenhouse, but smaller types do well outdoors. Keep an eye out for dwarf varieties such as 'Tumbler', which have been specially bred for growing in pots. Like the chillies, they also need regular feeding and watering.

Sowing a pinch of coriander seeds every few weeks during spring and summer will produce a regular supply of fresh leaves. If your plants do begin to flower, don't despair – not only are the white blooms very attractive, but you'll also get coriander seeds, which are equally useful in cooking.

TIP There is an amazing number of varieties of chillies from which to choose, but one good piece of advice is to check how hot the fruits promise to be – some can be absolutely scorching and you might find them inedible!

Salad in a trough

Plant an attractive container with lettuces and other salad leaves.

Time to plant: spring–summer

Salads are perfect crops for large pots and containers; they are quick and easy to grow and harvest. Salad leaves such as lettuces, chard and leafy mustards make trouble-free container plants. For one thing, they suffer less slug and snail damage than those grown in the ground, and they're easy to keep well watered, as long as the container is a good size.

Planters like this trough look great and the depth allows for plenty of compost, which will help the plants grow well. Place broken-up polystyrene chunks into the base of the trough, as this will improve drainage and reduce the amount of compost you need to fill it.

You could make it a complete salad in a bed by planting a few quick-growing crops such as beetroots and radishes alongside the lettuces.

TIP For best results, use young plants grown in modules, although you could sow seeds directly into a planter of this size.

Salad in a trough

Salsa!

Cabbages in crates

Grow big, leafy cabbages that are fit for kings. An old crate makes a good container to grow a couple of plants.

Time to sow: summer-hearting cabbages in early spring, winter-hearting cabbages in late spring, spring cabbages in midsummer

With their big, bold leaves and dense hearts, cabbages are remarkably attractive container plants. Grow them as mini-vegetables to be harvested when they are the size of a large cricket ball, but leave a couple to grow on to maturity.

Any good-sized container will do, as long as there is enough room to space the plants far enough apart, otherwise they will bolt. Large fruit crates lined with perforated polythene and filled with compost are ideal for growing about four plants: two to be harvested young and two to grow on. Make sure you choose really attractive varieties for the boldest, architectural look.

Good varieties include 'Ruby Ball', which is a beautiful red variety; 'Stonehead', a sturdy, green-leaved type.

TIP Protect from pigeons with netting, if necessary, and remove any cabbage white caterpillars as you spot them.

Mini runner beans

Dwarf varieties of runner bean make attractive container crops.

Time to sow: late spring

Pretty and productive runner beans grow well in a large container, and are happy to share the space with other crops or flowers.

Sow beans 5cm (2in) deep in modules or pots indoors and grow them on until the risk of frost has passed. In late spring or early summer, plant the seedlings up outdoors in a container filled with multi-purpose compost.

Space the plants about 10–15cm (4–6in) apart and provide a framework of twiggy sticks, canes or metal spirals for the beans to climb up. Underplant with trailing tomatoes, herbs or salads, or add a few flowers, such as climbing morning glory, for more colour. Water the container regularly, especially in hot weather.

Good varieties include dwarf 'Pickwick', which has red flowers and needs no support; 'Hestia', which has red and white flowers but needs pea sticks to scramble up.

TIP Feed occasionally with liquid fertiliser to give the plants a boost.

Blueberries in pots

Grow this 'super food' in pots for the best results.

Time to plant: spring

This fruit is ideally suited to growing in pots, as it needs a moist, acidic soil, which isn't found in many gardens.

Blueberries are a great, long-lasting and long-fruiting crop that should be planted in pots filled with ericaceous compost. They're reliably fruitful as long as they're watered with rainwater (which means setting up a water butt, if you don't already have one). The harvest is also considerably improved if you grow two or more blueberries that flower at the same time, as they will help pollinate one another.

Blueberries are attractive ornamental plants in their own right and often produce lovely autumn colours as the leaves fade. They are tough, hardy plants, but the spring blossom can be damaged by frost, so protect them with horticultural fleece if a cold snap is forecast. They also need regular pruning, as the fruits are produced on two- and three-year-old wood and you need to keep a steady supply of new branches coming. In winter, cut out any dead, diseased, or damaged stems, plus those that fruited the summer before.

Good varieties include 'Bluecrop', an early fruiter; 'Berkeley', a vigorous, mid-season cropper.

TIP Protect the fruits from hungry birds by covering them with netting.

A box of mini turnips

Make the most of your space by growing mini turnips – you can eat the tops and the roots of these tasty vegetables.

Time to sow: spring–late summer

Forget Baldrick's tasteless old turnips – these baby roots are fast growing and full of flavour. Tender, young baby turnips are a revelation to anyone used to tired, old roots cut into chunks in a stew. The seeds germinate within days, which makes this a great crop for the first-time veg grower. They grow Incredibly fast, too – the first sowings are often ready to harvest in around 6 weeks.

Turnips grow well in large containers, pots or even old fruit boxes filled with soil or a soil-based compost, as long as they're thinned to about 8–10cm (3–4in) apart. If they grow too close together they will bolt and produce no roots.

As they're closely related to cabbages, the new young leaves can be harvested as a tasty leaf vegetable in early–mid-springl, when other crops are still getting under way.

Good varieties include 'Purple Top Milan', which has tasty flat-bottomed roots; 'Snowball', which is perfectly white with a delicate flavour.

TIP It is essential to keep them well-watered to get them to produce a good crop, as turnips grow so rapidly.

Crops in grow bags

The perfect disposable solution for growing crops in small spaces.

Time to sow: spring–summer

Grow bags are a brilliant disposable method of growing crops in gardens where space is limited. They can even be used on balconies or put by the back door to provide fresh herbs and salads at arm's reach.

Although most often used for growing tomatoes, you can also use them as a complete mini-veg plot by cutting out the top of the bag – you can leave a couple of strips of plastic or add a binding of parcel tape around the middle to stop the compost spilling out and to separate varieties. Then sow directly into the bag or plant up with young plants. Salads, such as rocket, lettuces and mustards, and round-rooted carrots can all be grown in this way, as well as annual herbs such as dill and coriander.

Once the grow bag is planted up, if you have space, sow some more seeds in modules a few weeks afterwards and grow them on alongside. These can then be used to replace any plants you harvest from the grow bag, or any that die.

TIP Make sure you feed and water plants in grow bags regularly, as they will dry out quickly in summer.

Herb pyramid

Herbs are the perfect plant for growing by the back door, then within seconds of harvesting they are in the kitchen, ensuring their freshest flavours.

Time to plant: mid–late spring

To make the pot pyramid, start off with a wide container and fill it halfway with John Innes No. 3 compost. Adding extra grit to the compost gives the herbs the good drainage they enjoy.

Choose a second pot that, when placed inside the first one, will leave a band around the rim large enough to plant in. Fill in around the second pot with more compost, then repeat the process with a smaller, third pot.

Once you have your pyramid of pots, plant it up with your favourite herbs and put it in a sunny spot. Turn the pot regularly to give all the plants equal sunlight. Keep it well watered and it should provide regular harvests of fresh herbs all summer long.

TIP A pyramid pot creates a simple feature for a sunny site, but do plant it up in situ, as the completed display will be very heavy to move.

Crops in grow bags

Herb pyramid

Herbs in hanging baskets

Brighten up a dull wall with a glorious, aromatic basket of herbs, just asking to be picked.

Time to plant: late spring

Take advantage of a sunny house wall and plant up a fixed basket with a selection of your favourite cooking herbs.

Fast-growing leafy herbs make a pretty and practical hanging basket, and as long as they're within reach, you will even brave a spot of rain if you know you can quickly pick a handful. Any type of hanging basket will do: rustic woven ones are particularly fetching, and large wire ones with coir liners, like this one here, are readily available at garden centres and nurseries.

Choose herbs that you use all the time: moss-curled parsley, marjoram, sage and thyme are always good for cooking, and chives, chervil and coriander are great for spicing up salad leaves.

Water the basket regularly once it's planted, especially if it's on a sunny wall. Pick the leaves regularly, otherwise the basket will become overcrowded.

TIP Pop in a couple of nasturtiums for a splash of edible colour.

The 'three sisters'

Named by the Native Americans, the 'three sisters' – pumpkins, sweetcorn and beans – were grown together as the plants naturally help one another. Sweetcorn provides a climbing stalk for the beans; beans provide nitrogen to nourish the sweetcorn, and pumpkins cover the soil and help suppress weeds.

Time to plant: mid–late spring

Look out for dwarf varieties that are perfectly suited to growing in containers. 'Hestia' is an excellent dwarf runner bean that doesn't climb.

Alternatively, use dwarf French beans: you'll find colourful yellow and purple-podded varieties as well as the usual green ones. To keep their colour when cooking, microwave or steam them instead of boiling.

A delicious compact pumpkin perfect for growing in a pot is 'Baby Bear', which you harvest in autumn before first frosts.

As a final touch, add a few nasturtium plants; their colourful flowers will brighten up the area around the base of the sweetcorn, and when picked they will add a peppery flavour to salads.

TIP Use a container large enough to accommodate three or four sweetcorn plants. As they are wind pollinated, planting them in close proximity should ensure good pollination, resulting in well-filled cobs.

The 'three sisters'

Herbs in hanging baskets

Autumn fire

This fruitful gathering has great autumnal appeal, coming into its own in the latter half of the summer when many other containers are looking tired.

Time to plant: late spring–early summer

The centrepiece of this container, the chilli 'Apache', grows to only 45cm (18in) high but produces lots of small, medium-hot chillies that are highly ornamental and really spice up a meal. A colourful alternative is 'Fiesta', with fruits that vary from yellow and purple to orange-red.

The copper-brown grass, *Carex comans,* here creates a feathery backdrop, while the contrasting steel-blue leaves of *Koeleria glauca* and bronze uncinia grasses fill out the front of the container. Any combination of dwarf grasses would work equally well – try yellow-leaved *Acorus gramineus* 'Hakuro-nishiki' and blue fescue *Festuca glauca*.

Position a Lotus studded with orange-red blooms – to echo the chilli fruits – at the edge of the pot where its sea-green, needle-like leaves can cascade freely.

Plant up in late springwhen the danger of frost has passed, or any time during the summer. Plant the tallest grass at the back and the chilli in the centre, allowing it plenty of room to develop.

Place the container in a warm, sheltered spot to encourage the chillies to ripen.

TIP Start feeding chillies with a high-potash liquid feed as soon as the first flowers appear.

Wacky wellies

Containers don't have to be boring; all sorts of objects can be used instead of conventional pots – including cheap and colourful wellies! We've finished off the display with a watering can filled with veg, but use whatever object you fancy!

Time to plant: mid–late spring

To plant your wellies, start by drilling some drainage holes in the soles. These are vital as they allow excess water to escape. Then put some stones or pieces of polystyrene packaging inside further to improve drainage.

Support the legs of the wellies and stop them falling over by putting three canes inside each boot, cutting them so their tops are hidden when the compost is added.

Finally, fill the boots with multi-purpose compost and then either sow or plant your chosen veg. For an extra flourish you could even cut off the toe of the boot and squeeze in a drought-tolerant thyme.

TIP Wellies make surprisingly useful containers as their length gives space for roots to grow undisturbed. They are perfect for root veg such as carrots and parsnips, and long-rooted herbs such as chervil.

Autumn fire

Wacky wellies

Purple magic

Make the most of herbs with colourful leaves to create a pot that looks as good as it tastes.

Time to plant: spring

Dark green rosemary (*Rosmarinus officinalis* 'Blue Lagoon') takes centre stage in this dramatic container and gives height to the display. Its spiky leaves taste delicious with lamb and can also be used medicinally. 'Blue Lagoon' is a particularly pretty variety from early spring, when it is covered in deep blue flowers.

Silver-leaved curry plants (*Helichrysum italicum*) and purple-leaved sage (*Salvia officinalis* 'Purpurascens') alternate around the edge of the pot, interspersed with purple-flowered violas. Curry plants earn their name thanks to their amazingly pungent scent, although they're not actually used in curries. They make very ornamental plants, though, with their silvery leaves and yellow flowers.

Purple sage is another herb that is useful in cooking, and it tastes as good as the plain-green variety. The young leaves of this plant are dark purple, gradually fading to green as they age.

TIP This handsome combination of favourite herbs will last all summer. However, once plants begin to outgrow their space, simply move them out into the garden and replace with young plants raised from cuttings.

Culinary container

A practical take on an elegant container.

Time to plant: spring

A clipped bay tree makes an attractive container look good all year round, but if you underplant with shrubby herbs and flowers you can make a front-door feature a useful one, too.

Fresh bay leaves have a stronger flavour in cooking than dried ones, which makes this a great plant to have to hand. Evergreen bay trees look great when clipped into formal shapes such as cones and balls, and they grow extremely well in containers of all sizes for many years. They can be planted alone for a very formal look, or underplanted with more herbs as well as a few flowers to brighten up the show in spring and summer.

Try underplanting with rosemary, sage and thyme for the perfect array of culinary herbs, or grow with bedding plants such as pansies, pelargoniums and even pots of bulbs for a seasonal splash of colour.

TIP Trim formal bay trees back into shape in spring before they put on new growth.

Purple magic

Culinary container

Colourful Cape gooseberries

Cape gooseberries make an unusual and exotic container crop.

Time to plant: spring

Create a container that combines colourful, edible flowers with the dramatic papery lanterns of the ripening Physalis fruits. Cape gooseberry, *Physalis edulis*, is an easy and unusual container crop. You won't get masses of fruits (and they are a rather acquired taste, being quite sharp), but they look beautiful and they make an interesting garnish, or you can mix them with other fruits to make jams and tarts.

Grow physalis from seed, sowing indoors in spring, or buy young plants and start them off indoors, growing them on under cover until there is no longer a risk of frost. In late spring, plant outdoors in a large pot or recycled container, along with edible nasturtiums or marigolds for a real show of colour. Position the pot in a sunny, sheltered spot and water and liquid-feed with tomato feed regularly once the lanterns appear. Harvest in late summer/early autumn once the husks have turned translucent and papery, and the golden-orange fruit shows through.

TIP You can leave the ripe fruits on the plant until you need them.

Wild strawberries in wall pots

A container of dainty wild strawberries brightens up a dull corner.

Time to plant: spring

Alpine and wild strawberries are less demanding of rich soil and sunshine than their larger-fruited cousins. This makes them perfect container plants on their own or with other plants like the long-flowering, perennial daisy, *Erigeron*. They're also tougher and less prone to pests and diseases, and don't need netting to protect them from birds.

Wild strawberries flower and fruit beautifully all summer long, even in shady conditions. Grow them in pots and containers in a part-shaded spot and harvest the fruits to use as you would conventional strawberries.

Good varieties include 'Alexandra', which is juicy and enjoys a shady spot and moist conditions; 'Fraises des Bois', a classic, small-fruited type.

TIP Combine wild strawberries with conventional strawberries when making jam, for a fruitier taste.

Beetroots and carrots in pots

Grow root crops in containers for easy, trouble-free harvests.

Time to sow: spring–early summer

Producing long, straight carrots and blemish-free beetroots can be tricky in open ground. Both are favourites with slugs at the early stages of growth, and carrots can produce forked roots in stony soil.

Growing them in large containers overcomes these problems, as the young plants are well away from the attentions of slugs and a fine, free-draining compost should give you slender, fork-free carrots. Provided you water the plants well in the summer, you can also grow them closer together in the perfect conditions of a pot than you would in the soil, so even a small container can be surprisingly abundant.

Good varieties to grow together include beetroot 'Detroit 2 Little Ball', which is a bolt-resistant mini beet; carrot 'Sugarsnax', which is sweet and tasty.

TIP Get early crops by sowing a large pot of roots indoors in late winter to harvest as baby veg a few weeks later.

Tomato basket

Tumbling tomatoes produce a mass of stems that drip with cherry-sized fruits. Given the chance, a single plant will fill a hanging basket on its own, but here it is accompanied by curly leaved parsley and trailing black-eyed Susan (Thunbergia alata).

Time to plant: late spring

Yellow, orange and cream-coloured blooms of thunbergia will set off brightly coloured tomatoes to perfection. Its twining stems will also hide the basket chains and trail over the sides as it scrambles haphazardly through the tomato plant.

Parsley, the perfect herb for garnishing salads and all manner of other dishes, contributes a pool of fresh green leaves that should be picked young for the best flavour.

Pick the tomatoes as they ripen to encourage the plant to produce more fruit. Over the summer, gently train the shoots of the thunbergia in the direction you wish them to grow and trim away any leaves that shade the ripening tomatoes.

Fully laden with fruit, the tomato plant will be quite heavy, so make sure the basket is hung from a strong bracket.

Water daily, or twice a day if the weather is very hot or windy, and feed with tomato food once a week.

TIP Tomatoes and parsley are thirsty plants, so add a few water-retaining crystals to the compost when planting to reduce your watering chores.

Lavender and thyme basket

The beautiful herbs in this hanging basket will delight the eye all summer and are a treat both for the taste buds and nose.

Time to plant: mid–late spring

Choose a dwarf lavender such as the compact-growing 'Bella Series', which is available in a range of colours including white, pink and mauve-blue. Use several different varieties of thyme for a good mix of colour and flavour.

Lavender and thyme are both drought-tolerant, however, you will need to water the basket regularly, so add water-retaining crystals to the compost when planting and mix in slow-release fertiliser to keep them nourished. Remove faded blooms to encourage more flowers.

Position the basket in a sheltered spot, preferably where you can take a reviving sniff every time you pass by. At the end of the summer, plant out the thymes and lavender into a sunny, well-drained spot where they can give you years of pleasure.

TIP The chopped leaves and flowers of lavender can be added to biscuit mixtures to give them a distinctive taste and aroma, while thymes are excellent for bringing flavour to both meat and fish dishes, or in stuffing mixes.

Pots of potatoes

Potatoes will grow in almost any container and they make marvellous patio crops.

Time to plant: spring–midsummer

Plant in spring for early new potatoes and again in midsummer for a Christmas crop.

Potatoes will grow in pots, dustbins, specially bought potato barrels, and even black plastic bags, as long as the container is deep and has plenty of drainage holes. Place in a bright spot, put a layer of compost 10cm (4in) deep in the base of the container and place two or three chitted potatoes on top. Cover these with another 10cm (4in) layer of compost.

The wider the container, the more potatoes you can plant and the greater the harvest. A 30cm- (12in-) wide container will only hold one seed potato, but a 60cm (2ft) one should hold about three to five.

Keep the containers well watered. Once the shoots reach 10–15cm (4–6in) above the compost, add another 10cm (4in) layer of compost, leaving the tips showing. Keep doing this until the shoots are within 5cm (2in) of the top of the container. Harvest the crop when the flowers appear, by tipping out the container and digging in with your hands to uncover the potatoes.

TIP To grow a Christmas crop, it's best to move the container into a conservatory or greenhouse once the weather turns cold in autumn. Alternatively, move it into a sheltered spot near the house and cover the crop with fleece on frosty nights.

Lavender and thyme basket

Pots of potatoes

Courgettes in containers

Grow a single courgette plant in a pot for masses of vibrant flowers, foliage and fruit.

Time to plant: late spring

Courgettes are bold, fast-growing plants that look brilliant in large containers. The bigger the pot, the better, as far as a courgette is concerned; with their dramatic leaves and big yellow flowers, they can make quite a statement in a small space. Large pots, a wooden crate lined with polythene and even an old wheelbarrow all make good containers, or you can build a mini-raised bed with willow hurdles or pieces of wood.

Sow seed indoors in spring, but don't plant outside until all danger of frost has passed. Harvest the courgettes regularly once it starts fruiting – they'll soon turn into marrows if you don't – and keep the plant well watered, as courgettes are thirsty growers.

Good varieties include compact-growing 'Venus', with dark green courgettes; 'Gold Rush', with bright yellow fruits.

TIP For a taste of Italy, stuff male flowers (the ones without the swelling courgette behind) with ricotta and herbs, dip in batter and deep-fry them.

Grow mint in pots

Keep mint under control by growing it in a pot or container.

Time to plant: spring–summer

Mint comes in many different varieties and all the best ones grow brilliantly in pots.

There really is no other way to grow mint in a small garden than in a container. Most mints have incredibly invasive root systems, which means they can take over a small bed in no time at all. But despite their vigorous nature, they do grow well in large pots and containers, providing they have a sunny or slightly shaded spot and a rich, moisture-retentive compost. Ideally, mint should be planted on its own in a container, as it will rapidly take over a mixed pot of herbs. However, plants can die in pots, so to prevent the roots rotting, repot them every autumn using a soil-based compost.

For mint all winter, bring the pot indoors as temperatures drop, or you can root a cutting in late summer and grow it on in a pot on the windowsill.

Good forms of mint include Moroccan mint, which has a strong flavour and is the best variety for brewing as mint tea; applemint, which has furry leaves and a milder, delicate flavour that's good for cooking with peas. Eau de Cologne mint has bronze-green foliage and a strong, distinctive scent. It is ideal for a small garden, being hardy and responding to regular cropping with lots of new foliage.

TIP Pick regularly or clip to keep the plants thick and bushy and to encourage new shoots.

Grow mint in pots

Courgettes in containers

Step-over apples, page 49

Small beds and clever spots

Make your own raised beds

Raised beds look good and allow you to crop intensively. They are easy to construct and really make the most of a small garden.

Time to do: autumn–winter

Treated with wood preservative, raised beds should last for years. They have many advantages, including the fact that you can grow plants closer together in raised beds than in open soil, and that you can walk around the beds.

Walking over the soil to sow, dig, weed or harvest will cause it to compact, which causes problems for many crops, but root ones in particular. Aim to make each bed about 90–120cm (3–4ft) wide so you can reach into the middle of the bed without stepping on the soil. Make sure the paths are wide enough to walk through easily, or even to push a wheelbarrow through.

You'll need some long pieces of wood (Tanalised, if possible, as they last longer) to make the sides of the bed. These can be anything from 15–30cm (6–12in) high. You'll also need some sturdy, pointed stakes to fix the side pieces to. Measure the beds as accurately as possible and dig out the paths to mound up the topsoil in the beds. Hammer the stakes into the ground with a sledgehammer inside the corners of each bed – and also halfway down if the beds are long – then nail the sides on. Spread out the soil evenly across the beds.

TIP Keep your costs down by using recycled or salvaged wood, such as old railway sleepers or scaffolding boards.

Plan your space

Making a simple plan of your garden will help you think through ideas and maximise your space.

Time to do: autumn–winter

It's worth taking a little time to think about the design and layout of your garden before you get planting, as it's easier to make changes on paper than on the ground. You don't need to be a garden designer to draw a plan, simply start by measuring out the space, then plot it out on a piece of graph paper.

Once you have your basic layout, mark on it any permanent features such as trees, ponds, paths, and so on. Also include the house wall and mark where the back door is, and which way is north. This is essential so you know which wall is south facing and therefore sunny and warm – perfect for growing a grapevine or fan-trained peach tree. East- and north-facing walls are colder, shadier and better suited to growing a blackberry or hybrid berry.

Use this drawing as a template, make a few photocopies and play around with ideas, putting plants and beds in different places until you come up with something you like and that works for you and your space. Raised beds are ideal for small gardens as they contain your crops. You can also construct paths around them, which means you can tend crops without compacting the soil. Chunky timber beds, like those pictured opposite, can be a real design statement in their own right.

TIP Position a little bed for salad leaves near the kitchen door, or any other crop that grows quickly and gets used often.

Plan your space

Making raised beds

Plant thyme in gravel

This must-have herb for cooking takes up a tiny amount of space.

Time to plant: spring–early summer

Thymes need poor, well-drained soils to thrive and they love hot, dry sites. Plant them in a gravel path or in a sunny corner by a house wall and they'll be perfectly happy.

There are lots of different varieties, some tiny leaved and carpeting, others bushier and larger leaved, but all are good for cooking with. They also flower prolifically and, although the flowers are small, the plants become a mass of pink, mauve or white in the summer months. The flowers are also good for attracting pollinators such as bees into the garden.

Plants may need protection from winter wet, which can cause them to rot – covering them with a small cloche or a piece of glass raised up on bricks should do the trick.

Good choices include 'Minimus', which makes a tiny, dense carpet of leaves; lemon thyme, which has a lovely flavour; 'Doone Valley' with gold and green variegated leaves.

TIP Trim off all the flowers after they've finished to keep the plants bushy and to encourage new growth.

Chitting potatoes

Get potatoes off to an early start by chitting them before planting.

Time to do: spring

Chitting potatoes simply means encouraging them to sprout before they are planted, which gets them growing well before they go into the ground.

To do this, simply place the potatoes in an egg box or seed tray with the 'rose end' (the end with the most eyes) facing upwards. Keep them in a light place, though out of direct sunlight – for example in the spare room, kitchen, or by the shed window. After about 6 weeks the sprouts should be about 2.5cm (1in) long and the potatoes can be planted out into open ground or containers.

Good varieties include 'Cara', which is vigorous and crops well in a small space; 'Kestrel', which is unpopular with slugs.

TIP It is particularly beneficial to start early varieties off by chitting, as they have a shorter growing time than maincrop types.

Chitting potatoes

Plant thyme in gravel

Make a rhubarb patch

The perfect crop for a forgotten corner.

Time to plant: autumn or spring–early summer

Rhubarb really thrives in a sunny spot with a good soil, but it's very accommodating and will grow happily in a shady spot that you don't know what to do with. Once it has settled in, it will crop prolifically for years. Although rhubarb is not too fussy about site and soil, avoid planting it in waterlogged ground as the crown may rot.

Plant ready-grown plants in well-prepared ground, adding a generous helping of garden compost or organic matter. Allow the plant to grow for the first year and don't harvest the stems at all, as it needs to establish. Harvest only lightly in the second year and always leave a few leaves on the plant in following years to allow it to regenerate.

Good varieties include 'Champagne', with beautiful pink stems; 'Victoria', which is a strong grower; 'Timperley Early' which is a variety that holds the RHS Award of Garden Merit (AGM).

TIP Pick rhubarb between March and July as needed, or you can force it for an earlier crop (see p66).

Choosing small fruit trees

Get the right size tree for your garden.

Time to plant: autumn–spring

Small gardens need small trees to make the most of the space. There are hundreds of fruit-tree varieties available, many in a range of sizes. Most tree fruits are grown on specially developed rootstocks that can restrict the growth of the tree, making it suitable for the smaller garden or for growing in containers.

Look out for varieties labelled as dwarf or very dwarf. For apples, these tend to be the rootstocks called M9, which eventually makes a tree about 2–3m (6–10ft) tall and is used for dwarf bush and cordon types of tree, and M26, which grows to a final height of 2.5–4m (8–13ft) tall and is used for espaliers.

Step-over varieties – those low-growing forms that are trained horizontally as edgings for beds (see pp34 and 49) – are usually grown on the tiny M27 rootstock. Small pear trees, such as cordons, espaliers, and dwarf pyramid types, are nearly always grown on Quince C or Quince A rootstocks (see p66).

Good varieties include apple 'Sunset', which has a lovely flavour; pear 'Conference', which is reliable and hardy.

TIP If you only have room for one tree, try a 'family' apple tree – it has two or three varieties grafted on to one plant.

Making a seedbed

It really pays to take time to prepare your ground well before sowing seeds.

Time to do: spring–autumn

As a rule, the finer the seeds, the better worked the ground needs to be in order for them to germinate and grow well. Carrot seed, in particular, is very fine and needs a well-prepared bed, otherwise the seeds become buried under clods of earth and can't reach the light. Beans, however, have huge seeds that will thrust their way through all but the densest soil.

Every autumn, if you are between crops, dig some well-rotted manure into the bed (unless you are using the bed for root vegetables – see right). Break up any large clods of soil and compost as you fork over the bed thoroughly. Use a flat-headed rake – the heavier the better – to even out the soil in the bed and to remove any stones or twigs, or any weeds. Hand-pick out any persistent weeds.

Using the rake again, gradually work the soil into a fine 'tilth' – a lovely breadcrumb structure that is perfect for sowing seeds.

TIP Always use a line to mark out seed rows if your beds are long – it is much easier to hoe between straight rows of plants later on.

Improving your soil

Feed your soil, and your plants, and you'll be rewarded with abundant crops.

Time to do: winter–spring

A healthy, rich soil bursting with nutrients is bound to produce good crops. Adding plenty of organic matter while forking or digging over the beds in winter and spring will keep your soil fertile and moisture retentive for the coming season. (See p57 for tips on how to make your own compost.)

Dig well-rotted manure, garden compost or leaf mould into clay soils in winter, but leave sandy soils until spring, otherwise all the nutrients will be washed away in the winter rains. Always stack up manure and leaves to rot down thoroughly. Never use fresh manure as it's too strong and could kill your plants or, at the very least, take essential nitrogen from the soil as it rots down.

TIP Adding manure to areas where you intend to grow root crops such as carrots and parsnips will produce forked roots if the soil is too rich.

A space for figs

Figs love a sunny wall and will grow well with very little root space.

Time to plant: winter–spring

As long as the space is big enough to dig a hole, a fig will grow well. In fact, they often do best if their roots are restricted, as otherwise they can become hugely bushy and leafy, and bear little fruit.

Fig trees need plenty of sunshine and a really warm spot, as the fruits take all summer to develop. Keep the plant pruned back within the space each spring, and use wires and canes to train the branches flat against the wall or fence, tying them in with twine.

Remove all the larger figs that haven't fully developed each autumn, leaving the little embryo figs to grow and ripen the following summer.

Good varieties include 'Brown Turkey', which is very hardy and a prolific cropper; 'White Marseilles', which has beautiful translucent flesh.

TIP Plant in the ground, lining the sides of the hole with vertical paving slabs and filled to within 20cm (8in) of the top with broken bricks to restrict the roots.

Make compost with a wormery

In a small garden, a wormery offers a compact, space-saving way to make excellent compost and liquid fertiliser.

Time to do: all year

A wormery allows you to make great compost and fertiliser simply by letting worms munch through all your household food scraps and peelings. These leftovers would attract vermin if put on the compost heap, but an enclosed wormery turns this waste into rich compost. In addition, the liquid drained off from the base of the wormery makes a brilliant liquid fertiliser when diluted with water.

You can buy purpose-built wormeries or make your own from an old compost bin, buying the worms from mail-order companies or using ones from an existing compost heap.

Worms will eat almost anything, but don't add too much food in one go – allow the worms to process the material a layer at a time. Don't add fish or meat waste, seeds or citrus peel, as the worms won't be able to digest these.

TIP Site the wormery in a shady place to stop it getting too hot or drying out, and keep it covered to prevent flies becoming a problem.

A space for figs

Make compost with a wormery

Plant veg around the patio

Get the most from your space by planting veg among your flowers.

Time to plant: spring–early summer

Pretty and productive vegetables and herbs can add a splash of foliage and fruit colour to beds and borders around the garden or around a patio. In small spaces, this proximity means that picking fresh ingredients is just an arm's length away.

Many herbs and vegetables grow well when planted with ornamental plants and can help to fill planting gaps throughout the season. They need the same conditions as many border flowers, and with plenty of sunshine, water and good soil, they perform well and can be just as attractive.

Beetroot, coloured-leaved chards, the clustered rosettes of lettuces, carpets of thyme or low mounds of sage look stunning mixed in with annual flowers and bedding plants. For added drama, use mini-sweetcorn and train dwarf beans up little obelisks.

Good varieties include beetroot 'Bull's Blood', which has rich, dark red leaves; sweetcorn 'Minipop', which produces baby corn cobs perfect for stir-fries.

TIP Keep sowing more pots of lettuces and salads so you can replace those you harvest and avoid creating gaps in your border.

Grow fragrant fennel

Florence fennel grows swiftly and makes a good crop for a small space, as the bulbs, feathery leaves and seeds are all edible.

Time to sow: late spring–early summer

Florence fennel needs a sheltered, sunny site to grow well. It does require a little planning and attention, though, as It is prone to bolting if plants are grown too close together or lack regular watering.

Sow the seeds where they are to grow and cover them with fleece to improve germination, as they don't like temperatures to be too cool. You can remove this fleece in June or July, or whenever the weather settles into a long warm spell.

Thin the seedlings to 25–30cm (10–12in) apart and water to settle the soil. Keep them well watered in dry spells and harvest a few leaves whenever you need them. For bulbs, grow on until the bulbs reach tennis-ball size, which is when they're ready to harvest.

Good varieties include 'Zefa Fino', which is resistant to bolting; 'Perfection', which is ideal for early sowing.

TIP Allow a few plants to flower, as they'll attract beneficial insects. The seeds are also good in baking.

Plant veg around the patio

Grow fragrant fennel

A wigwam of runner beans

Runner beans romp away once they've germinated, rapidly covering a wigwam, wall or trellis, or filling a container.

Time to sow: late spring–early summer

Sow individually in pots to a depth of about 5cm (2in) indoors or in the cold frame, or directly into the ground outside from late spring, allowing 15cm (6in) between plants. Transplant seedlings outside, into the positions where you want them to grow, when all risk of frost has passed.

Put wigwam frames or poles in place before you sow or plant outside, and train climbing varieties up their supports as they grow. This is particularly important if you are growing several plants, as beans grown in blocks tend to crop more heavily. Alternatively, train on to a trellis, arch or frame as an attractive and productive screen.

Keep runner beans well watered as they flower, and pick the beans when young for the best flavour, as this will help keep the crop coming.

Good varieties include 'Painted Lady', which has beautiful red and white flowers; 'Red Rum', which has red flowers.

TIP Remember that this is a warm-climate crop, originally from Mexico, so don't be tempted to plant it outside too early.

Doubling up

Nasturtiums give pumpkins a floral pick-me-up.

Time to sow: nasturtiums late spring–early summer, pumpkin seeds indoors early spring. Plant out in May

Pumpkins and squashes are perfect in pots, but the plants are a little dull and take up too much space to warrant growing them on their own. Of course, the end crop is delicious, but these plants take several months to reach maturity and all you have to look at during this time are some massive, but not particularly pretty, leaves.

This failing is easy to remedy. Simply sow a few trailing nasturtium seeds in the container when you plant out the pumpkin or squash. The nasturtiums will grow quickly, tumbling down the sides of the pot or climbing through the pumpkin plant, using its stems as supports.

As well as creating a striking show of colour, nasturtium flowers are also edible. They have a peppery taste and are perfect for brightening up a summer salad.

TIP Pumpkins are good in a redundant corner, where you won't walk on the trailing stems. Grow in a 25-litre pot and keep well watered. If the fruit sounds hollow when you tap it, it should be ready for harvesting.

Doubling up

A wigwam of runner beans

Carrots in beds

The flavour of home-grown, freshly pulled carrots is second to none.

Time to sow: mid-spring–late summer

Growing your first batch of carrots every year is a delight. You can start the season off early by warming the soil with cloches. The secret to good carrots is a well-prepared, light, sandy soil that they can push their roots easily into without forking.

Dig and fork the bed through a couple of weeks before planting and rake the soil to a really fine texture. Hoe off or hand-pick out any weeds that appear, without disturbing the soil too much, then sow the small seeds thinly, following the spacings on the packet, and barely cover them with soil. This should reduce the amount of thinning you need to do later – which is good news because it's the smell of carrot thinnings that attracts carrot root fly, probably their worst pests. (See pp133 and 188 for tips on dealing with these pests.)

Good varieties include 'Sweetheart', which is tasty and yields early crops; 'Flyaway', which has some resistance to carrot root fly; 'Parmex', which is a ball-shaped carrot that grows well in heavier soils.

TIP Don't be tempted to sow outdoors too early in the season, as carrots need warm temperatures to germinate.

Dig out perennial weeds

Get your crops off to a good start by clearing your beds of perennial weeds early in the year.

Time to do: winter–spring

Before you get sowing, you need to be sure that the area is not only clear of annual weeds but also of perennial weeds, otherwise these will suddenly appear again and again and be unwelcome competition for the growing crops.

These weeds will compete with crops for space, moisture and nutrients in the summer. They are difficult to dig out without disturbing the roots of your crops, so it's best to clear them out thoroughly when digging over the bare ground in winter and spring. It is also easier then because the soil tends to be moist and the roots can be lifted cleanly without breaking them.

Perennial weeds, such as docks and dandelions, have deep roots that can re-grow if any part is left in the ground, so you need completely to remove all the roots when weeding.

TIP Do not compost the roots of perennial weeds – chop the leaves off and compost these, but burn or bin the root systems.

Blackberries on walls and wires

A true sight and taste of autumn.

Time to plant: autumn–spring

The attractive, apple-blossom flowers of a blackberry look lovely in summer and the fruit, synonymous with autumn, is perfect for pies and jams.

Blackberries are very fruitful and forgiving plants, as they will tolerate a shady spot and even a frost pocket – although a sunny, warm site will result in more fruit. They make an attractive flowering and fruiting plant for a wall or fence, and can be easily trained along wires, although the thornless varieties are much more pleasant to handle.

Allow plenty of space when planting, as the stems are very long, and position the horizontal wires about 30cm (12in) apart, training each stem up and down in a sort of weave as it grows.

Good varieties include 'Loch Ness', which is thornless and very prolific; 'Oregon Thornless', another thorn-free variety, which has attractive, deeply cut leaves.

TIP Blackberries are very tolerant of wet, clay soils, but if you have a sandy, light soil you'll need to add plenty of organic matter to retain moisture.

Step-over apples

You can find room for this tiny tree in even the smallest garden.

Time to plant: autumn–spring

Step-over apple trees are ideal for small-space gardening. An apple tree is a must-have for any keen fruit grower, producing fruit reliably as well as adding blossom and colour to the garden.

Step-over varieties are trained to be low growing, only reaching about 45cm (18in) tall, and need to be pruned annually in winter to keep their shape. A framework of canes allows the branches to be tied in securely, and although they don't bear as much fruit as larger trees, they should still produce enough apples to make their care worthwhile. And they'll all be within easy reach for picking!

Plant the trees in a row at the front of a border to act as a miniature, fruitful hedge. Choose a sheltered spot, as the blossom can be damaged by late frosts, and prepare the ground well, adding compost or organic matter to the planting hole.

Good varieties include 'Egremont Russet'; 'Fiesta'; 'Sunset' and many others.

TIP Aim to plant two or three varieties that flower at the same time, as this will improve pollination and ensure a good crop.

Buying ready-grown plants

If you haven't the time or space to bring on seedlings, using young vegetable plants is the perfect solution.

Time to do: spring–late summer

It may cost more than seeds, but buying packs of young, healthy plants is handy if you're really short of the space and time needed to grow your own seeds. They are widely available from nurseries, garden centres, and mail-order or online from specialist seed companies or veg growers throughout the season. Young plants are an especially good option when it comes to plants that you only want a few of and that need warm, steady temperatures to germinate, such as tomatoes, chillies, cucumbers and peppers.

Young plants are also very handy for filling in a few gaps as the season wears on, and also for experimenting and trying something new. However, you don't get the range of varieties that are available from seed, and root crops such as beetroots and carrots shouldn't be bought this way as they don't like being transplanted.

TIP Buy young plants of tomatoes and peppers in a few different varieties to see which ones you prefer.

Grow your own garlic

Growing garlic is easy and rewarding, producing a reliable crop.

Time to plant: autumn–early winter

Plant garlic from mid-autumn to early winter, as it needs a period of cold to stimulate growth. Always buy your first planting of bulbs from a garden centre, nursery or mail-order catalogue, as supermarket garlic, which is for eating rather than planting, tends to grow poorly. You can then save some of your own bulbs for growing in subsequent years.

Plant cloves of garlic in a sunny spot. Make sure each clove has its own bit of the root base-plate attached, and sow it 8cm (3in) deep and 15cm (6in) apart. You can also grow a few bulbs in large containers, if that's ll you have room for. Leave them to do their thing, but occasionally push cloves back into the soil if birds have tugged them out of the ground. Harvest bulbs once the leaves start to yellow from early summer onwards, and dry them off in a cool, dry place before storing.

Good varieties include 'Thermidrome', which is specially selected for the UK climate; 'Early Purple Wight', an early maturing garlic with purple bulbs.

TIP If the plant produces a flower stem, nip it off to increase the size of the bulb.

Buying ready-grown plants

Grow your own garlic

TLC for plants and soil

Keep soil healthy by growing each type of crop in new places every year.

Time to do: winter

When the weather turns cold and the new seed catalogues are delivered for the year ahead, spend some time thinking about where you will grow next year's crops. You will get a better harvest if you don't plant the same type of vegetable in the same place every year. Changing their locations helps to combat pests and diseases within the soil and can even increase its fertility.

Crops also utilise different trace elements in the soil. If you grow the same thing year after year, your soil will gradually become impoverished in certain trace elements. Herbs are very sensitive to this and appear to lose flavour in tired soil, especially tarragon and mint, so it's a good idea to move them around beds or repot them every so often if they are in containers.

To do this successfully in a small garden, keep your beds fairly small for ease of rotating. Having 4 small beds makes the system much easier to implement (see p118), then you can rotate the different groups of plants among them as best you can every year.

TIP Plant potatoes in the weediest section, as their leafy growth will shade out the worst of the weeds.

Companion planting

Growing specific plants alongside vulnerable crops can help ward off pests without having to resort to chemical controls.

Time to plant: spring–summer

If you are keen to garden organically, particularly when it comes to food crops, you won't want to resort to chemicals and pesticides every time a pest comes along and attacks your plants. Non-chemical sprays and solutions are available, but one really natural way to deter pests in the first place is by 'companion planting'.

This method involves interspersing certain crops with specific plants that will provide a beneficial effect. This occurs in a variety of ways, from masking crops with a pungent aroma, visually hiding plants, or producing flowers that attract and feed benefical insects like hoverflies.

French marigolds and nasturtiums help to keep brassicas free from cabbage white butterflies, and they also help to deter whitefly from tomatoes. Florence fennel can help to attract beneficial predators such as lacewings into the garden, while many fragrant annual herbs, such as dill and chervil, are said to boost the growth and flavour of lettuces and other salad leaves. Perennial herbs such as rosemary and lavender ward off many pests, while leeks and onions planted in between rows of carrots deter carrot fly.

TIP Choose plants such as French marigolds and nasturtiums for the dual purpose of adding colour to a small garden and protecting plants from pests.

Companion planting

TLC for plants and soil

A pretty and productive patch

Small beds and lots of flowers can create a practical and attractive space.

Time to plant: spring

A potager is an ornamental vegetable garden where herbs, flowers and vegetables are grown in small beds as much for their good looks as their crops.

Herbs such as lavender and chives are traditional in these types of gardens, as are plenty of edible flowers and attractive foliage crops, such as ruby chard and lettuces. Flowering beans, golden-fruited courgettes and fruit bushes also look lovely, and you might even find a sunny spot for a globe artichoke plant, which produces huge, purple, thistle-like flowers.

Beds can be at ground level or raised; they look great with an edging of wooden planks, woven willow, bricks, or even low box hedges.

Good varieties include anything colourful, such as ruby chard, lettuce 'Pandero', and nasturtium 'Tom Thumb Mixed'.

TIP Underplant taller plants such as fruit bushes with flowering herbs, including chives, coriander and chervil.

Beautiful baby beetroots

Fast-growing beetroots look and taste lovely and they make a really useful quick crop among longer-term veg.

Time to sow: spring–late summer. Plant out seedlings in modules once well rooted

Beetroots come in a wide range of shapes and colours – not just the usual red globes. Varieties with golden or striped roots are particularly attractive, but there are also tapered varieties and even a pure white form, which is useful as it won't stain your clothes when you chop it up.

Start sowing in spring under cloches and keep going until midsummer, as baby beets can be harvested at ping-pong ball size after about 8 weeks. For pickling, let the beetroots grow for longer until they reach 5cm (2in) in diameter. Make repeat sowings directly into the ground if you have room, or sow into modules and plant out as young plants.

Good varieties include 'Detroit 2 Little Ball', which is deep red; 'Burpee's Golden', which is orange; 'Barbabietola di Chioggia', which has pink roots with white rings. All young, tender beetroot leaves are excellent for adding to salads, but if you want them specifically for this purpose, sow some 'Bull's Blood' and you can pick from the same plants all summer.

TIP The corky seeds of beetroot contain inhibitors, which slow germination, so soak the seeds for half an hour before sowing.

A pretty and productive patch

Beautiful baby beetroots

Espalier apples and pears

Trained fruit trees take up little space and look beautiful.

Time to plant: autumn–early spring

Covering a wall or fence with an espalier-trained tree takes a little time but doesn't require a lot of space. Looking after an espalier apple or pear may sound difficult, but if you keep up with the winter shaping and pruning it's straightforward and hugely rewarding. You can train your own or buy ready-grown espaliers at specialist nurseries or good garden centres; they will crop more quickly but will cost more than an untrained tree.

To train a young tree, first fix wires horizontally to the fence or wall about 35–45cm (14–18in) apart. Plant an unfeathered maiden tree (that is, a very young one that hasn't branched yet) and remove the leading shoot above three good upper buds. The two lower buds should then each produce a shoot that goes along the wire, in opposite directions, in the summer. The following winter, train in these shoots along the wire and allow the new leading shoot, the third bud, to grow up. Carry on in this way until you have the required number of tiers – it will take a few years. In between this winter training, prune in midsummer, shortening all side shoots to encourage flowering wood to develop at the base.

Good varieties include pear 'Doyenné du Comice', with a glorious flavour and large fruits; apples 'Egremont Russet' and 'Lord Lambourne'.

TIP Always plant at least 15cm (6in) away from the fence or wall to allow room for the trunk to grow.

Thinning and spacing between plants

Getting the spacing right between developing seedlings early on gives plants a great start.

Time to do: all year round

However carefully you sow, seedlings will nearly always need thinning out to ensure each plant has the space it needs to grow to its full potential. The correct spacing for individual varieties will be found on the seed packet of whatever vegetable you are growing, so do use this as your guide.

It's easy to sow larger seeds, such as beans and peas, the right distance apart. Young plants sown in pots are also simple to space out correctly when transplanting outside. However, tiny seeds like carrots, radishes and parsnips always end up too close together and must be thinned out. If they aren't, plants tend to become stressed and fail, or they run quickly to flower and seed without producing a crop. Many root vegetables are especially prone to this if left too crowded.

Thin by carefully pulling all the unwanted seedlings from a row, leaving the strongest plants the correct distance apart. Always water the remaining seedlings after thinning out, to settle the soil.

TIP Use your hand to hold down the soil around those seedlings you want to keep, as you pull the others out.

Fruitful French beans

These beans offer a big harvest in a very small space. Varieties with attractively coloured pods are ideal for the potager or in containers.

Time to sow: spring–midsummer

Beans are easy to grow and extremely fruitful for the small-space gardener. Grow climbing types up a wigwam of canes (see p126) or against a fence on a wooden or cane trellis. Dwarf varieties can be grown in pots and containers, or interplanted between slower-growing brassicas.

You can sow seeds outdoors from mid-spring until midsummer. Sow them 5cm (2in) deep in the ground, or in pots indoors or in a cold frame in early spring. Dwarf varieties are best spaced 20cm (8in) apart in rows 20cm (8in) apart, and climbing types 15cm (6in) apart with 60cm (2ft) between rows. Keep the plants well watered when in flower to help the pods set, and pick the crop regularly to ensure the plants produce more beans (see p132).

Good varieties include climbing 'Cosse Violette', which has purple pods; 'Opera', which has plentiful crops of green beans and is resistant to many bean diseases. 'Cobra' is another practical choice for small gardens as it produces a heavy crop of tasty green beans over a long season. For really small spaces, try dwarf 'Sprite' for its green pods; 'Purple Queen' for its tasty purple pods.

TIP French beans are self-pollinating, so planting them close together produces better crop.

Composting in a small space

Compost is a fantastic source of nutrients for your beds – and making your own is a good, free way to turn spent plants into something useful.

Time to do: all year round

Garden compost is a valuable source of organic matter and nutrients, which are essential for growing good vegetables, especially if you're cropping more intensively in raised beds. You should add organic matter to most beds every year so the soil doesn't become depleted of nutrients. Although you can always buy manure, using your own garden compost is much more satisfying.

Even in small gardens you can make your own compost, there are specially designed bins for every space, or you can make your own.

You can put most things on the compost heap, such as grass clippings, debris from crops and other plants, but avoid adding any diseased plant material, as diseases can survive in a small-scale, relatively cool heap. Household kitchen waste, such as vegetable peelings and tea bags, can be thrown in too, but don't use cooked foods, as these tend to attract vermin.

TIP Compost bins come in all shapes and sizes. If you want to buy one, contact your local council first as they often sell them at a discount.

Grow a strawberry wall

Clothe a dull wall with delicate flowers and luscious fruit.

Time to plant: spring

The classic fruit of the summer makes a pretty and productive use of wall space. Strawberries will grow in just about any container, as long as they have a rich soil with plenty of organic matter or garden compost mixed in, and they don't get too hot and dry.

A sunny, sheltered wall is the perfect spot for tubs, wall containers and tiered troughs. As with any container, make sure you water regularly – every day in the heat of the summer and twice daily in high temperatures if they are in hanging baskets. On a weekly basis, add a high-potassium liquid fertiliser such as tomato feed.

After the last crop has been picked, remove all the old foliage and fruit stems, and give the plants one last good feed. Leave them outside over winter and they will crop well the next year, but do replace strawberry plants with new young plants every four years.

Good varieties include 'Cambridge Favourite', which is reliable and delicious; 'Flamenco', which produces fruit for a long period over the summer.

TIP Protect developing and ripening fruits from birds with netting.

Grapes on a sunny wall

Bring a touch of the Mediterranean to your garden with a juicy grapevine.

Time to plant: early spring

Train a grapevine on a sunny wall for a delicious, fruitful climber. They are easy and attractive to grow, with lots of vigour and plenty of lush leaves.

Pick your spot carefully, as grapevines can get quite big, although they're brilliant for brightening up a dull fence or pergola, especially in autumn when the leaves turn lovely orangey-red colours. They're tolerant of poorer soils and, as long as they have a warm, long autumn, can fruit remarkably well. Keep vines well watered in dry spells when they are fruiting, particularly if they are growing against a wall or fence and thus sheltered from rainfall.

Strict pruning is a must, otherwise the plant will be all foliage and no fruit. Aim to create an open framework of branches, and prune each shoot back to a few leaves after the flower truss. Make sure you protect the developing fruits from hungry birds by covering the vine with netting.

Good varieties include 'Boskoop Glory', with rich, dark grapes; 'Maréchal Joffre', which produces good-sized fruits.

TIP Thin some grapes from the bunches as they develop, to reduce the chance of mildew and encourage individual grapes to grow larger.

Grapes on a sunny wall

Grow a strawberry wall

Grow gooseberries in shady corners

If you have a cool, shady spot in your garden, try growing gooseberries.

Time to plant: winter

Although you'll probably get more fruit in a sunny spot, gooseberries are very tolerant and will produce excellent crops in a shady site. A couple of plants make good use of that difficult corner, but avoid planting where it is cold and frosty, and make sure they're sheltered from cold winds in spring when the plants are flowering, otherwise the crop could be ruined.

Allow plenty of room per plant, as each one can spread to 1.5m (5ft) wide, and prune in winter to stop it encroaching on paths and other plants. Feed it with a high-potash fertiliser in spring to encourage good fruiting.

If space is tight, gooseberries can be either bought or trained as half-standards or cordons, which can be squeezed into the tiniest of plots. With a bit of careful pruning of sideshoots and nipping off the top of the main shoot, you can get a good harvest from just one stem.

Good varieties include 'Pax', which is virtually thornless and also shows good resistance to American gooseberry mildew; 'Leveller', which has a lovely flavour.

TIP So-called thornless varieties still have some spines but are much easier to pick than the painful thorny types.

Edible flowers

Use these flowers to add colour to the garden and your salads.

Time to sow: spring–summer

For centuries edible flowers have been used in salads and drinks to add colour and a hint of flavour. Annual plants such as pot marigolds (calendula), nasturtium and borage are easy to grow and will often seed freely around the garden, providing you with flowers for years to come.

Sow the seeds in situ directly into the ground, or in individual modules or pots to plant out where you want them. Dot them around in gravel paths, or at the edges of beds to soften hard lines and add a 'cottage garden' feel to your design.

You can pick whole nasturtium blooms and calendula petals to use in salads, while borage flowers are traditional in Pimm's and lemonade. You can even freeze borage flowers in water in ice-cube trays, which you can add to drinks as a pretty garnish.

Good varieties include calendula 'Orange King', with bright orange flowers; nasturtium 'Alaska Mixed', with multi-coloured flowers and marbled leaves.

TIP Deadhead spent blooms regularly to encourage the plants to keep flowering. Stop doing this towards the end of the summer, though, so you can collect seeds for next year.

Grow gooseberries in shady corners

Edible flowers

Juicy gooseberries, page 75

Fruit

Pick pears in their prime

There's something wonderful about biting into a freshly picked pear that's so ripe it sends juice running down your chin. But how can you be sure that your pears are ready for picking?

Time to do: late summer–autumn

When they are ready to pick, the fruit should still be quite firm, although not rock hard, and with most varieties the skin colour becomes a slightly paler shade of green.

If you are uncertain, carefully cup the fruit in your hand and gently, but firmly, give it a slight twist. If it is ripe, the fruit stalk should break from the spur and you'll be left holding a delicious pear.

For some early varieties the bite test is probably the most reliable way of seeing if the fruit is ready for eating. Pick the fruit and take a bite. If it is still hard and relatively flavourless, then wait a week or perhaps more before trying again.

When picked, bring them into a warm room to ripen, or store in a cool space for later use – but don't store in polythene bags, as this encourages rot.

TIP Try stewing peeled whole pears and eating them with a hot butterscotch sauce spooned over. Delicious!

Give melons a go

One of the most refreshing fruits to eat on a hot summer's day is a melon, with its sweet, juicy flesh. Although the melons we buy from supermarkets are grown in warmer climes, it is possible to grow your own in a greenhouse.

Time to sow: late spring

Melons are closely related to cucumbers and require similar growing conditions to thrive. The secret to producing good fruit is not to sow the seed until late spring when the days are warmer, and the plants will develop much faster.

Melons need warmth, water and food to grow well. They can be quite vigorous, so regular pruning is needed to keep them under control and ensure they put their energies into fruiting, not foliage.

Grow plants in containers 30cm (12in) in diameter. Plant the melon in the centre on a low mound with the compost level graduating down. This helps to prevent water standing around the base of the stem, which can lead to rotting. Help the fruiting process by hand-pollinating the flowers. Strip the petals from the male flower and rub against the female flower (the one with slight swellings behind the flowerheads).

Provide plants with a support to grow up and water regularly and feed on a weekly basis. Thin out the tiny fruits to leave a maximum of four melons per plant.

TIP Look out for small cracks appearing around the stalks of melons – this will tell you that your fruit is ready to harvest.

Give melons a go

Pick pears in their prime

Choose the right rootstock

Fruit trees are propagated on to rootstocks; this is the most important factor in determining the vigour and eventual size of the tree.

When choosing your fruit tree, you will need to make sure you buy one on the right rootstock so that you get a tree that is most suitable for the size of your garden (see p40 for rootstocks for small spaces). The tree will have been joined ('grafted') on to a suitable rootstock, as varieties do not breed true from seed.

For plums, 'St Julien A' is a semi-vigorous rootstock suitable for most soil conditions, including relatively poor soil and grassed orchards. A mature tree will reach 3–3.6m (10–12ft) with a spread of 3.6m (12ft). If you want a smaller tree, try the dwarfing rootstock 'Pixy' which reaches 2.5–3m (8–10ft), but this is only worthwhile on good soil.

Apple trees are grafted onto 'M9', the most popular dwarf rootstock; 'M27', which is the smallest but requires very fertile soil; 'M26', which gives a compact tree, or 'MM106', a larger, orchard-size tree.

Most pear trees are grafted on to quince rootstock. 'Quince A' rootstock is the most popular. Trees grafted on to this will reach 3–6m (10–20ft) high. You'll also find pears on 'Quince C' rootstock, but these trees won't grow quite as large, as the growth slows once the tree starts to produce fruit. 'Quince C' trees will also fruit a fortnight earlier than other rootstocks.

TIP If you can't wait for your pears, try 'Quince C' trees, as they will fruit a fortnight earlier than other rootstocks.

Get early rhubarb

There is something immensely comforting about rhubarb, especially when it is buried beneath a thick layer of crumble and custard.

Time to do: early to midwinter

Rhubarb is a delicious treat that can be enjoyed as early as late winter or early spring by forcing crops. This involves keeping the plants in the dark, which encourages an earlier crop of tender sticks.

Forcing is easily done using traditional terracotta rhubarb forcers, or even a black plastic dustbin. The important thing is to get your forcer of choice in place over your rhubarb plant by midwinter.

When the crop, whether forced or not, is ready, always pull the stalks rather than cutting them. You may feel that you are removing pieces of the plant in the process, but doing it this way hugely reduces the risk of the plants developing potentially fatal rots.

Save your sharp knife to cut off the foliage and the white end of each stick while you are in the garden and add them to the compost heap.

TIP 'Valentine' is a great variety as it has a delicious flavour and very tender stalks. Other varieties worth growing include 'Champagne' and 'Stockbridge Arrow'.

Choose the right rootstock

Get early rhubarb

Prune raspberry canes

Once the very last of the summer-fruiting raspberries have been eaten, it is time to set to and sort out the canes. Cut down to ground level all canes that have borne a summer crop of fruits, which will allow plenty of space for the newer canes to produce their crop next year.

Time to do: autumn and spring

Choose seven or eight sturdy, healthy-looking canes per plant, then train them into the system of support wires. Space them well so that each has plenty of room – a distance of 8–10cm (3–4in) between them works well. Snip out the remaining canes with secateurs.

Tie the canes into position using garden twine. Invariably some of the canes will be taller than the top wire, but rather than cutting these off, loop them over and tie them back into the top wire. They should be cut back to about 15cm (6in) above this wire in late winter. It may sound crazy doing it this way, but if pruned back in late autumn the canes tend to fruit less well the next year, so that extra bit of twine tying is time well invested.

TIP Autumn-fruiting raspberries, such as 'Autumn Bliss', are even easier to prune than summer-fruiting varieties; simply cut back the canes to ground level in late winter.

Making fruit jams

Preserve bumper crops of home-grown fruit by making jam with them.

Time to do: summer–autumn

Soft fruits always seem to ripen at the same time – strawberries, currants, plums and gooseberries – all delicious and all needing to be used swiftly before they spoil. Making jam is a wonderful way to preserve the fruit and enjoy its flavour all year round. It takes a little effort, but is very rewarding and you can have fun trying different combinations.

Large amounts of fruit also disappear into tiny jars, which make far more sense for storing, and you and your friends and family don't get fed up with seasonal gluts of soft fruit.

All you need to make jam is an equal quantity of fruit and preserving sugar and plenty of sterilised jars. Boil the fruit and a little water for 10 minutes, then add the sugar and boil for another 10–15 minutes. Drop a little jam on to a saucer cooled in the fridge; if the surface of the jam wrinkles when prodded, it is ready, if not, boil for another 5 minutes. Put the jam into jars, seal, and they can be stored in a dark cupboard for up to a year.

TIP Try making apple jams first to get your hand in, as these often set very readily.

Summer pruning

Peaches, nectarines, plums and damsons all perform better when pruned in summer.

Plant bare-root fruit trees

Bare-root plants are available from late autumn to early spring and offer a cheap way of buying fruit trees.

Time to do: spring–summer

Spring and summer is the best, if not only recommended, time for pruning plums and damsons, as they are prone to silver leaf disease, which can infect them if they're pruned in winter. As with other fruit trees, start with any damaged, diseased or dead branches first, and then only prune further if absolutely necessary.

In spring, on peaches and nectarines, simply rub off with your finger and thumb any shoots that are growing in the wrong direction – towards the wall or fence on fan-trained trees, for example. Then, in summer, pinch out the new shoots you don't need to create a framework of stems about six leaves long.

After cropping, these pinched-out shoots can be trimmed back to three leaves to stimulate fruiting buds to form next season.

TIP For fan-trained trees, train in new stems every year to fill any gaps in the framework.

Time to plant: late autumn–early spring

Dig out a large enough hole to accommodate the root system, and fork over the base, mixing in some garden compost and bonemeal. Take your fruit tree and spread out the roots well in the planting hole. Add your tree stake now to minimise damage to the roots.

Backfill the hole with a mix of topsoil, garden compost and bonemeal, checking regularly that the stem is not being buried too deeply. This is because the graft point must be kept above ground level, otherwise the graft could fail or the tree could produce growth from the rootstock instead of the upper portion. (The graft point is a distinctive lump on the stem, just above the roots.)

Once the tree and stake are in place, firm the soil around them well with your boot (but not too hard if the soil is heavy), and check the level one last time. Finish off by giving the plant a thorough watering and make sure it is well watered for the next few months.

TIP Lay a straight bamboo cane or small plank across the top of the planting hole to align with just below the graft point to check that the planting depth is correct.

Fruitful small plots

Even the smallest garden can squeeze in a fruit tree or two if they are trained in a fan shape, so that they lie flat against a fence or wall.

Time to plant: late autumn–early spring

Fan-training a fruit tree not only means it takes up the least amount of space but also provides it with extra protection from the elements – helping more sensitive fruits, such as peaches and nectarines, produce successful crops. It is also easier to protect a fan-trained tree with netting or fleece than a free-standing one.

When and how to prune depends on the type of fruit, but for sweet cherries like the one in the picture opposite, it's worth choosing two or three shoots on each branch and tying them in to fill any gaps in the framework. Pick shoots that will be easy to train in this way, then prune out the rest.

On more established fans, you will also need to tie in suitable shoots to fill gaps. Prune back the shoots that you don't need to about five or six leaves. Do this in summer, before you put netting over the tree to protect the fruit from birds.

Feed your tree in early spring with sulphate of potash to promote flowering and fruiting, then again as soon as the fruits begin to ripen.

TIP You can have a go at fan-training your fruit trees, or you can save yourself the work and buy trees that have already been trained.

Protect fruit blossom

The sight of a fruit tree covered in blossom in spring is breathtaking, and this makes them worthy of a place in the garden.

Time to do: spring

Blossom is very susceptible to frost, so you must provide cover if it is forecast. If frost damages the blossom you will not only lose the flowers, but it can also have a disastrous effect on the crop.

Draping horticultural fleece over a fairly small tree works well, and if you want to keep it that bit more snug, use a double layer. You can even use old net curtains. Wherever you live, but especially if your garden is subject to fierce winds, make sure that you anchor the fleece well.

Pollinating insects will still need to reach the blossom, so the fleece or other covering must be removed each morning, then replaced as necessary. It may be time consuming, but it's well worth the effort.

TIP Whatever you use to protect blossom, make sure it is permeable and will allow moisture out and air in. A solid layer, such as polythene sheeting, causes a lot of problems with muggy, damp air and condensation.

Fruitful small plots

Protect fruit blossom

Make room for raspberries

Choose a couple of varieties with different fruiting times and you can enjoy juicy raspberries from summer until first frosts.

Time to plant: spring or autumn

Raspberry canes should be planted by early spring. It pays to ensure that the soil has been well manured in advance. If the soil is heavy, then incorporating plenty of grit should improve drainage, or you could try planting the canes on a slight mound.

Summer-fruiting raspberries need a sturdy support system of tanalised posts with struts and galvanised training wires. It is easiest to get this in place before planting. Autumn-fruiting raspberries form a denser thicket of canes than their summer cousins.

Always choose healthy-looking canes – preferably those certified as being virus-free – and plant them 38–45cm (15–18in) apart, with about 2m (6ft) between the rows. It is important to spread their roots well so that they will form a plentiful supply of new canes. Once the canes are in position, cut them back to about 25cm (10in) above soil level.

TIP 'Glen Moy' and 'Glen Prosen' are all great summer-fruiting varieties, while 'Joan J' and 'Fallgold' will extend the harvest into autumn.

Root new strawberry plants

Strawberries are one of the most delicious fruits of the summer garden. After a few years, though, plants tend to become less productive, but they can be easily and cheaply replaced.

Time to do: late summer

Strawberry plants are ridiculously easy to grow. They thrive in a sunny spot and the only other real requirement is that the compost is kept moist at all times.

Once strawberries have finished fruiting, in late summer, clear away the straw from around the plants. Now you can easily get at the 'runners' – the small plants sent out on long shoots by the parent plant. Choose a runner with healthy green leaves and, leaving it attached to its parent, pin it on to the surface of a pot filled with multipurpose compost. A U-shaped staple, or a piece of wire, is perfect for holding it in place.

When the new plants are strongly rooted and living an independent life, they can be severed from the parent plant. Remove them from their pots and plant them in their new home in the ground, or plant into larger patio pots and baskets (see p148).

TIP When planting strawberries, press the soil down around the roots. To test if they're planted firmly enough, gently tug one of the leaves; if the plant lifts from the ground, replant it more snugly.

Make room for raspberries

Root new strawberry plants

Feed and weed

Your soil is still moist and just starting to warm up in spring, which makes it the perfect time to mulch around the base of fruit plants.

Time to do: spring

Remove any weeds and gently dig over the soil surface (if it is compacted) before applying mulch. A thick layer of mulch nourishes the plants and also reduces the amount of weeds reappearing in spring.

Lay a mulch of manure, compost or other suitable material in a circle about 45cm (18in) in diameter – or even wider if you have the space. Provided the soil is moist when mulched, this blanket will help reduce moisture loss from the soil and will also insulate beneath the soil surface.

It is important not to smother the plants when adding a layer of mulch around them, and it must not touch the stems or trunks as this could encourage diseases, stem rotting and generally make the plants struggle.

When you've finished mulching, not only will the plants benefit but your beds will also look neat, tidy and well cared for.

TIP Raspberries in particular really benefit from a good mulch. Their roots are especially vulnerable to drought as they sit near the surface of the soil, where the ground is driest.

Preserve your fruit crop

So you've harvested your fruits and this year's bumper crop could feed an army, but if you pack it away and preserve it, you could be eating home-grown produce all winter.

Time to do: summer–autumn

Some fruits are perfect for storing in the freezer, especially raspberries. Lay them out individually on a tray, making sure they're not touching, and freeze them overnight. Once frozen you can put them in an airtight plastic box and they will stay separate; unlike strawberries, they won't turn to mush once they've thawed. This method also works well for currants, blackberries and gooseberries.

Apples and pears are best stored immediately after harvesting – although don't bother with early varieties of apple as these don't keep well. Select only unblemished fruits, rejecting any with bruises, holes, or signs of disease or pest attack.

Ideally you should wrap each piece of fruit in a piece of greaseproof paper and place it in a wooden slatted box so that air can circulate around it. Or place apples in a plastic bag pierced with several holes.

Leave the fruit in a cool, dark place and it should keep for several months. Check it every so often and remove any fruits that show signs of going off.

TIP Use up gluts of fruit by blending them into juices or smoothies. Drunk fresh, they're packed with healthy vitamins and anti-oxidants.

Juicy gooseberries

Gooseberries are one of the easiest fruits you can grow, producing heavy crops of green, yellow or red fruits even in their first year.

Time to plant: autumn–spring

As soon as the crop is just about ready to pick, consider netting the bush in order to keep those succulent berries for your own use, rather than have the whole lot consumed by the local bullfinch population. Over smaller plants, hold the net in place with bamboo canes topped with inverted flowerpots to keep it in position. Always ensure the net is firmly anchored at the base, otherwise the birds may find a way in at ground level.

Drenching the soil around the bush with water on a regular basis will help produce larger fruits. Around 25–50 litres (5.5–11 gallons) per square metre (square yard) should keep the roots moist for a good while, especially if the soil is covered by a mulch. Be regular with your watering and keep the moisture supply coming consistently at the roots once the fruits are ripening – erratic watering will cause your gooseberries to split.

Good varieties of gooseberries to look out for are 'Invicta' and 'Whinham's Industry'.

TIP A moist soil will help to keep your gooseberries free from powdery mildew, which covers the berries in a white coating.

Strawberries from seed

The traditional way to raise strawberries is to root runners (see p72), but if you don't have plants from which to propagate, raise them from seed.

Time to sow: early–mid-spring

Great varieties of strawberries are available as seeds at a fraction of the cost of plants; if you sow them in early spring, you should get fruits the same year.

Early sowing is essential for the best crop in the same year, but remember that strawberries are perennials so they will flower and fruit again for several years. Sow any time between early and mid-spring in a heated propagator in your greenhouse or on a windowsill – setting the temperature at 18–21°C (65–70°F) for the best germination.

Strawberry seeds are very small, so take care when tipping them out into your hand. Dampen a finger to pick up a few seeds at a time and sow on the compost surface.

Pot up seedlings into 8cm (3in) pots, keep them in a greenhouse or cold frame and feed weekly as they develop. Once plants are looking sturdy with a good rootball, plant them outside in an open, sunny position. Growing strawberries in large pots seems to help deter slugs.

TIP You'll find a range of different varieties on sale in mail-order catalogues and in the garden centre. Tiny alpine strawberries are particularly sweet (see p28).

Jewels of summer

Grow a selection of currants along with strawberries and raspberries and you can create the most delicious summer puddings and jams, or just enjoy handfuls of fruit fresh from the plant.

Time to plant: late autumn–early spring

Redcurrants, whitecurrants and blackcurrants have to be among the prettiest fruits you can grow. Redcurrants in particular look like clusters of jewels as they weigh down the branches. They are easy to pick off the plant and can then be removed from those irritating twiggy bits using a fork.

Site plants in a sheltered position, away from cold winds in spring when the plant is flowering, as this can hinder the formation of fruit. Make sure you can reach the plant, for ease of picking, and are able to cover it. Currants ripen fast, so unless you are quick off the mark, or have them properly netted or in a fruit cage, the birds will often get there first.

TIP Look out for the following varieties: redcurrants – 'Red Lake' and 'Jonkheer van Tets'; whitecurrants – 'Versailles Blanche' and 'White Grape'; blackcurrants – 'Ben Lomond' and 'Ben Sarek'.

Pretty as a peach

Fan-train a peach tree against a wall or fence for a feast of fruit and flowers.

Time to plant: winter–early spring

Peaches respond well to training and will produce a reasonable crop on a sunny, south-facing wall or fence if their stems are pruned and tied in to a fan-shaped framework. If you don't have suitable wall space, there are also several varieties available as dwarf versions. These can be grown in containers as small trees, but will produce full-sized peaches.

Peach trees are happy in a well-drained soil, but need mulching every spring to make sure the roots stay moist through the growing season. The plants are fully hardy, but their blossom needs protection from frost as they flower very early in spring. If a cold snap is forecast and the plant is in bud or flower, cover it with horticultural fleece. The other downside to this early flowering is that pollination is difficult without many insects around, so you may need to hand-pollinate trees.

Establishing the basic framework of a fan does take one or two growing seasons, depending on the age of the tree that you buy, but after that pruning and other maintenance are very easy. You will also need to hand-pollinate flowers with a brush then thin out any fruits as they appear.

Good varieties include 'Peregrine', which produces lovely yellow-white fruit; 'Rochester', which is tasty with yellow-fleshed fruits. 'Avalon Pride' is a new variety that is naturally resistant to peach leaf curl.

TIP Protect developing fruit from hungry birds by covering with netting.

Jewels of summer

Pretty as a peach

A shady corner for raspberries

A cool, shady corner is the perfect spot for growing raspberries.

Time to plant: winter

Just a handful of raspberry bushes will fruit steadily and reliably for about 12 years, if they're given the right start. They need a rich, fertile soil with plenty of organic matter dug in before planting, and a good mulch at the start of the growing season.

Grow a few plants in a shady corner by a fence or as a screen (see p72). Set up a framework of posts and wires and tie in the stems as they grow. Protect the ripening fruit from birds with netting draped over the frame.

Raspberries are available as summer- or autumn-fruiting varieties, so if you're a big fan of the fruit, extend the cropping season by planting one of each.

Good varieties for shady spots include 'Glen Ample', which is a summer-cropping type with masses of tasty fruits; and 'Autumn Bliss', which is a favourite late-fruiting variety.

TIP Raspberries will cope with heavy shade providing the soil isn't poor and dry.

Success with strawberries

A few weeks of warm weather in late spring, combined with some of that omnipresent rain, is enough to get strawberry plants moving at an incredible rate.

Time to do: spring–summer

With a plentiful supply of healthy, bright green foliage, fresh flowers will open daily and more and more fruits will form. Inspect both the flowers and the fruits regularly, and if any are showing signs of problems, pinch them off.

Frost is the main danger for strawberry flowers. If you spot a damaged fruit, remove it promptly so the plant does not lose energy and so that the remaining fruits can benefit.

Once the strawberries start to form in earnest, place a thick layer of dry straw beneath each truss of fruits. This holds them clear of the ground, reducing slug and snail damage, and it also helps to keep the fruits clean. On heavy-cropping varieties, so many trusses form that it's best simply to put straw down over the entire area to start with. You can buy special strawberry mats, but they are often too small and tend to buckle, which means they don't retain moisture in the way a thick straw mulch does.

TIP If you live in a frost-prone area, protect your plants by covering them with cloches or horticultural fleece.

Success with strawberries

A shady corner for raspberries

Growing mint, page 87

Herbs

Try something different

Rosemary is an interesting herb in its own right – it looks lovely, smells marvellous and tastes great. It is also an evergreen plant.

Time to plant: spring–autumn

There are some lovely varieties to look out for, one of the better known ones is *Rosmarinus officinalis* 'Miss Jessop's Upright', which has pale blue flowers and a very upright habit. If you fancy another colour rather than blue, then there is a white-flowered form, *R. officinalis* var. *albiflorus*, or you could try the pink-flowered *R. officinalis* 'Roseus' or 'Majorca Pink'.

It is not only the flowers that can vary, but also the growth habit of the plants. *R. officinalis* 'Prostratus' Group is a trailing variety that has pale blue flowers, while the stunning, blue *R. officinalis* 'Fota Blue' has arching stems.

The scent of the leaves can also vary. *R. officinalis* var. *angustissimus* 'Benenden Blue', for example, has a very piney scent, while *R. officinalis* 'Green Ginger', as its name suggests, has a hint of ginger.

TIP Visit a specialist herb nursery to see – and smell – the full spectrum of varieties.

Take cuttings

Buying plants can be a costly business, so take a few cuttings of your favourite herbs to get extra ones for free.

Time to do: spring–summer

The best time of year to take cuttings is in spring or summer, when the plant has plenty of new, leafy growth.

Select a healthy shoot that doesn't have any flowers – such as the sprig of applemint pictured opposite, below. Make a sloping cut with a sharp pair of scissors or a knife, just under a pair of leaves. Remove the bottom leaves, as these would rot if left on when the cutting goes into the compost.

Mix perlite or grit into a multi-purpose compost, to make it free-draining, and fill a module tray or pots. Use a dibber or pencil to make a hole in the compost and insert the cutting. Gently firm it in.

Water the cuttings and place them on a well-lit windowsill. Plant the cuttings out into individual pots when they have rooted.

TIP Rosemary, mint, thyme and sage are ideal herbs for propagation by cuttings. If you have any spares, swap them with friends and family to fill your herb garden.

Try something different

Take cuttings

Save your seed

Saving seeds from your herbs is an easy way to enjoy home-grown plants – it is great fun and very rewarding, both inspirationally and financially.

Time to do: late summer–early autumn

Late summer and early autumn are the ideal times to start collecting seeds. By then many plants have produced seed heads that are becoming brown and dry, and this is their signal to you that they are ripe.

Choose a dry, preferably sunny, day, so the seeds are as dry as possible. Arm yourself with either brown paper envelopes or boxes lined with paper or kitchen paper (to absorb any moisture), sticky labels and a pencil.

Remove the whole seed head using secateurs or scissors, but don't snap it off because this can cause you to lose a lot of seeds. Collect seeds in separate envelopes or boxes, taking care not to mix them up. Seeds encased in berries should be collected as soon as the berries are just over-ripe.

TIP It's easy to forget which seeds are which by the time you get indoors, so label them as you go. Add the date before storing, so that you know how old they are and whether they are still viable when you come to sow them.

Growing supermarket basil

Basil is definitely one of the most rewarding herbs to grow. It's an attractive plant that comes in many shapes, sizes and colours, and is grown all over the world.

Time to plant: spring

There are many types of basil, all of which are edible, and all have a different flavour. It's a wonderful culinary herb and its versatility in the kitchen is matched in the garden, where striking purple basils make superb spot plants at the front of a warm border.

All basils make excellent companion plants, and the reliable bush varieties are great planted throughout the vegetable garden, as they repel a number of pests.

Supermarket basil is raised quickly (22 days from seed to sale), so the rootball is underdeveloped compared to conventionally raised plants. This is why supermarket basil (the left-hand plant in the picture opposite, top, alongside a home-grown basil) normally dies if it is planted out in the garden. If you want to keep supermarket herbs going, divide them with care and repot in light compost. Keep the compost moist but don't let it dry out. Place in a warm position until the plants are fully rooted. They should then grow on like seed-raised basil.

TIP Basil is known for repelling house flies, so it's ideal for growing in containers positioned outside your kitchen door.

Growing supermarket basil

Save your seed

Sow herbs in a grow bag

Grow bags are generally associated with greenhouse crops such as tomatoes and sweet peppers, but they are also great for growing herbs.

Time to sow: late spring–early autumn

Leaf crops grow best when positioned in partial shade, as this prevents the leaves scorching in the midday sun. It also helps stop the grow bag from drying out. (There should be instructions on the bag about making holes for drainage.)

Cut two large windows in the plastic to give you the maximum sowing area for your crops. Once the bag is opened, use a fork to fluff up the compost. Water the bag well, then use a pencil or length of dowel, pressed horizontally into the compost, to mark out your sowing lines. In a standard-size bag you can have up to six rows.

Late spring is the ideal time to start sowing outside, and you can continue sowing until early autumn.

To guarantee pickings over the winter months, put the grow bag in a cold greenhouse from early autumn onwards.

TIP Tape the grow bag in the middle prior to cutting – this will give it extra strength when you cut the openings.

Divide herbs

An easy way to increase the quantity of herb plants, including oregano and mint, is to divide an established clump.

Time to do: spring or autumn

To divide a herb, simply dig up the parent plant and split it into pieces, each with its own roots and leaves.

Some plants can simply be pulled apart, such as oregano, but others are harder to break up. If that's the case, either insert two garden forks back to back in the centre of the clump and lever them apart, or get an old bread knife or a pruning saw and cut through the clump. It may look brutal, but the plant will soon recover.

Replant the new pieces as soon as possible after the plant has been divided. Alternatively, pot them up until you're ready to put them in the ground. Keep them well-watered for the first few months after planting while they establish new roots. The new plants will soon put on growth until they are eventually big enough to be split apart themselves.

TIP This technique can be used with many ornamental plants as well, such as hostas and phlox.

Growing mint

One of the most popular of all herbs is mint. It has been used for hundreds of years to flavour food, sweets, toothpaste and medicines, and comes in a tempting array of flavours and forms.

Time to plant: spring–autumn

Mint can be used fresh, scattered over green or fruit salads, or chopped up and added to mayonnaise or salad dressing. It can also be cooked with vegetables such as peas to bring them to life. Alternatively, use it to add a heavenly minty flavour to chocolate mousse.

Some particularly flavoursome varieties include mild-flavoured gingermint, *Mentha* x *gracilis* 'Variegata', which has gold and green leaves, chocolate peppermint, *M.* x *piperita* f. *citrata* 'Chocolate', which has dark brown leaves that taste rather like After Eights, and red mint, *M.* x *smithiana*, with red stems and green and brown tinted leaves that have a good spearmint flavour.

Renowned for being invasive, you should plant mint with care. The best-flavoured and healthiest plants are those that spread naturally, so plant them in rich, well-drained soil, in a sunny spot where they can grow unrestricted. If space is an issue, however, plant mint in containers to control it (see p32).

TIP Cut back hard after flowering for a fresh supply of leaves in early autumn.

Plant great garlic

Garlic is an essential ingredient in so many dishes, so it's brilliant to have your own supply just outside the kitchen door.

Time to plant: autumn or spring

Garlic thrives in a sunny spot in well-drained soil, but it will also grow in heavier soils provided the drainage is improved. This is easily done by planting the bulbs on a 13–15cm (5–6in) high ridge of soil and adding grit if necessary.

You can plant garlic bulbs in spring, but planting in autumn will achieve the largest, plumpest and earliest crop (see p50).

A good variety is 'Vitesse', which has a beautiful purple-pink flush and is ready by early summer. It is also wonderfully tasty when harvested a few weeks early and stores for 4–5 months. 'Ivory' is also good; it is a pure white variety ready by mid-summer. Its real asset, apart from its wonderful taste and aroma, is that it stores until late spring.

TIP Only plant garlic that has been specifically produced for growing and is certified virus and eelworm free. Using leftovers from your vegetable rack is likely to result in virus problems.

Herbs in pots

Many herbs thrive in window boxes and other containers.

Time to do: spring–summer

A pot or two of mixed herbs placed just outside the kitchen door is always handy when you are cooking, and most herbs love the growing conditions of pots and containers.

Give herbs free-draining compost and a warm spot in the sunshine all summer long and they should thrive, especially annual herbs such as basil, parsley and summer savory. Many shrubby perennials, such as rosemary and thyme, are quite happy in pots for several years and can provide a winter garden with much-needed evergreen structure.

Rather than planting them singly, try grouping herbs together in a pot. Team perennials such as rosemary and marjoram together, then grow annuals such as basil and parsley in a separate pot, as they'll be easier to look after that way. Take cuttings of the herbs and bring them on, so when the plants start to outgrow their space, you can replace them with new, home-grown plants.

TIP Plant any shrubs and perennial herbs that will be in the pots for several years in a soil-based compost, mixed with grit for improved drainage.

The secret of sowing parsley

Parsley is one of those all-round useful plants that no herb garden should be without. There are many superstitions associated with sowing parsley, but it's really not that tricky to grow a good crop.

Time to sow: spring

The most important factor in sowing parsley seeds is not to allow them to dry out during germination. If sown in early spring under protection – at around 18°C (65°F) – germination should take 2–4 weeks. Alternatively, sow the seed in a prepared site in late spring when the night temperature does not fall below 7°C (45°F). Seeds should germinate in 2–4 weeks.

Parsley is a hungry plant that likes a good, deep soil, not too light and not acidic. Always feed the chosen site with well-rotted manure in the previous autumn.

Parsley is ideal for container growing, and it should thrive indoors on a windowsill as long as it is watered, fed and cut regularly. You could also try growing it in a hanging basket, but it must be kept well watered. Alternatively, try it in a window box, but do give it some shade in high summer. When growing parsley in a container, allow enough room for the tap root to develop.

TIP Parsley makes an ideal companion plant when sown with vegetables. It is said to keep onion fly away and to deter carrot root fly. Parsley also grows well with tomatoes and will flourish when sharing their feed.

Herbs in pots

The secret of sowing parsley

Prepare a brew

If you like to keep your herbs close at hand for a really fresh brew, why not grow some in fun, tea-themed containers in your kitchen?

Time to do: May–September

What you grow is up to you – lemon balm will perk you up if you're feeling tired, and is said to relieve headaches and tension, and restore memory. Lemon verbena has relaxing properties and is particularly refreshing as an iced tea on a hot summer day. Thyme is an antiseptic, good for mouthwashes and even hangovers!

Sow or plant the herbs in standard plastic pots that can be dropped into and lifted out of the containers easily. You can start off with potted herbs from the supermarket while you wait for your sowings to grow.

When you want a brew, simply put a handful of fresh herbs into a mug, pour over boiling water and leave to infuse for five minutes.

TIP For more herbal tea ideas and their health benefits, turn to page 94.

Know your tarragon

There are three herbs commonly called tarragon – all are herbaceous, have mid-green narrow leaves and a distinctive aniseed flavour.

The Rolls-Royce of tarragon is the French one, *Artemisia dracunculus*, with its distinctive aniseed flavour that is renowned in Béarnaise sauce and chicken and tarragon dishes. French tarragon can transform roast chicken into a feast and makes soups and sauces a digestive delight.

Russian tarragon, *Artemisia dracunculus* subsp. *dracunculoides*, has long oval leaves with a slightly bitter flavour and only a hint of aniseed; it is commonly used in Persia as a salad plant. It is very hardy and has attractive sprays of tiny yellow blooms in summer.

Winter tarragon, *Tagetes lucida*, is from Mexico and has coarser, larger leaves than its cousins. It dies back in spring rather than winter, hence its common name. Winter tarragon has a very strong aniseed flavour and so it is better used in cooked dishes, especially with roast meat or vegetables and in soups.

TIP French tarragon is the only type worth preserving. The quickest and easiest method is to make an infusion with fresh leaves and white wine vinegar, which can then be used to make salad dressings and sauces.

Prepare a brew

Know your tarragon

Bundle up a bouquet garni

There is nothing more comforting on a cold winter's day than tucking into a casserole that has been cooked with fresh herbs. This is how food used to be enjoyed, and so it can be today.

Time to plant: summer–autumn

By using fresh herbs in your cooking, you can create a wonderful and healthy meal, and key to these dishes is the bouquet garni, which means 'a bunch of flavouring herbs'. These are commonly used to enhance the flavour of soups and casseroles, which are usually cooked in a single pot.

The origins of the bouquet garni can be traced back to medieval times when meals were cooked in a pot over an open fire and the green vegetables were known as 'pot herbs'. A few herbs still retain the name 'pot' in their common name, such as pot marjoram, *Origanum vulgare*.

A mixture of herbs, including bay, lemon thyme, lemon balm, lemon grass leaves, rosemary, summer savory, hyssop, thyme, tarragon and parsley, is excellent with chicken. Or use any combination of fennel, lemon balm, French parsley, mint, sweet marjoram, tarragon, a small sprig of lovage, dill, Welsh onion stems and bay with fish. If you want to flavour a meat-based casserole, then try using a selection of oregano, thyme, bay, lovage, rosemary, sage or parsley.

TIP Use a long piece of undyed string to tie your herbs together, as this makes it easy to remove the bouquet garni at the end of cooking.

Make more of your crop

Freezing and drying work well as ways of preserving herbs for use later in the year, but to get a little something extra from them, try making herb butters and vinegars to capture the delicious taste of fresh herbs.

Time to do: summer

To make a herb vinegar, pick lots of sprigs of your favourite herbs and submerge them in as big a drum of white wine vinegar as you can get your hands on. It's best to blanch them first (plunge the sprigs into a mug of boiling water to kill any possible bugs), then leave them to steep for a month in the vinegar before straining.

Herb butters also make great use of any excess harvest. To make a butter, take a good handful of any soft green herb, such as chives, tarragon and parsley, and add it to two pats of soft butter, mixing it all together in a food processor. Remove the mix, place it on some cling film, roll it into a cylinder and freeze. Cut off discs as and when you want them to put on top of steaks or carrots.

TIP Herb butters and vinegars are incredibly useful in flavouring a wide range of dishes, and a bottle of home-made vinegar is a perfect present.

Herbs for shade

It's a generally held belief that herbs prefer full sun, especially the Mediterranean types such as thyme, sage and oregano. However, herbs such as chervil, parsley, salad rocket and coriander actually benefit from being grown in partial shade.

Time to plant: spring–autumn

Herbs that prefer shady conditions are happier there because they hate the soil drying out in summer. They produce better leaf crops if they're not subjected to the midday sun and, because the soil doesn't dry out as rapidly, they're less prone to bolt (flower quickly) and will therefore continue to produce leaves for a longer length of time.

Keeping such herbs in partial shade can result in softer leaves that have a more subtle flavour. This is a real advantage with some herbs, such as sorrel, which becomes tough and bitter when it is grown in full sun. On the other hand, shade is not good for mint or chives, as it can cause them to grow leggy. If you regularly cut their leaves, you can keep them under control and encourage them to produce new growth.

TIP Avoid growing sweet marjoram, summer savory and cardoon in shade. They grow so weakly in cool spots that they keel over and become food for slugs and snails.

Time to harvest

Harvesting herbs regularly not only benefits us, but it also helps keep the plants productive and healthy. However, there's a right and a wrong way to harvest them, so to get the most from your herbs it pays to know how they grow.

Time to do: all year round

Herbs grow in one of two ways: by producing leaves along a stem, or by shooting stems up from the base or crown. Stem-grown plants include bay, thyme and mint, while crown-forming examples are chives, parsley and rocket.

Leafy herbs should be nipped off where the leaf meets the stem, while crown-forming herbs should be taken right back to near the base of the stems using scissors or a knife – think of it as pruning on a small scale. Get it right and you'll have sturdy, long-lasting plants that will keep you supplied all summer. Get it wrong, and it's goodbye to your crops.

To harvest successfully you need to know how to pick herbs, and also when to do it. For those with succulent leaves, such as basil, pick before flowers are formed. Once this process starts, all the plant's energy goes into producing blooms and then seed, and the leaves become tough and sour.

For evergreen herbs such as sage, cut off the flowers and give the plant a good trim in late summer for a second flush of leaves that will provide you with succulent pickings through autumn and winter.

TIP Harvest annuals such as parsley before they run to seed; after this they won't produce any new leaves.

Freeze fresh herbs

During the summer and early autumn many herbs put on a phenomenal amount of growth, and supply can outstrip demand. Drying is the traditional method of preserving herbs, but freezing them is also well worth trying.

Time to do: summer–autumn

A whole range of delicious herbs can be frozen successfully, including parsley, basil, thyme, oregano and chives.

Select only the healthiest, freshest shoots and cut them off cleanly. Wash, then carefully chop into small pieces. Pour water into an ice-cube tray, filling it a quarter full, then pack each cube with the chopped herbs, ensuring that as much of the leaf as possible is covered by water. Top up the tray with water just to below the rim.

Put the tray in the freezer, keeping it level, and leave it to freeze. This method ensures they hold on to their flavour because they are frozen when fresh.

These herbs are now easy to use: when a recipe requires a particular herb, simply take a cube or two and pop it straight into your saucepan. Drop these herbs into casseroles and sauces while they are cooking and, as the ice melts, your dishes are infused with the delicious flavour of home-grown herbs.

TIP Save yourself time and hassle – decant the frozen cubes into labelled bags and put them back into the freezer. Then when you need a herb you know exactly where it is and can take it straight out of the bag.

Make a herbal tea

As we all try to reduce our caffeine intake, we are advised to drink herbal teas. Try a cup of your own home-grown herb tea and you'll be amazed at the flavours.

Next time you feel bloated after a meal or have an attack of indigestion, try a cup of peppermint tea. Simply put a handful of fresh or dried leaves into a teapot or mug, pour over boiling water and allow it to stand for 5 minutes with a lid on. It's important to keep it covered because the evaporating steam carries the essential oil. When you drink it, the warmth, flavours and aromas of the tea help you to relax, while also easing that bloated feeling.

A cup of fennel seed tea can ease the pain when you are suffering from wind or stomach cramps. Place one teaspoon of seeds in a teacup, pour over boiling water, let it stand, then strain and drink. Fennel seeds are also very beneficial when chewed after a rich or spicy meal, as they help freshen the breath and settle the stomach.

A tea made from hyssop leaves is an excellent tonic if you are suffering from a cough and cold, as it is a gentle decongestant and expectorant. However, avoid drinking it if you are pregnant.

TIP If you're suffering from the effects of the night before and have a big day ahead of you, brew yourself a cup of fresh rosemary tea – it helps to stimulate the memory and clear a hangover. For an interesting way to store herbs and for more tea ideas turn to page 90.

Make a herbal tea

Freeze fresh herbs

Make a lavender bath bag

Lavender is one of the most useful herbs to aid relaxation. Not only generally regarded as a tonic for the nervous system, it is also a potent sedative and calming remedy.

Time to do: summer

Lavender is particularly effective in helping to relax you and soothe your nerves when added to a bath – as a few drops of lavender oil or as fresh or dried lavender flowers.

To make a lavender bath bag, place a handful of dried blooms in a square of muslin. Take the four corners of the muslin and tie them together securely with string. Make a loop to hang it from the bath tap. Allow the hot water to run through the bag. This will not only scent the water, but also fragrance the whole room.

TIP The fragrance of lavender produces a calming response, so plant it beneath windows or around seating areas. Then you can sit, breathe it in and exhale gently at times of stress or at the end of a long day.

Soothe the skin

Using plants directly on the skin to ease pain or treat surface ailments is an age-old practice – and a very effective one. So why not grow your own natural remedies and have a pharmacy on your doorstep?

Time to plant: all year round

Aloe vera is a remarkable plant for its healing powers, both internally and externally. In the 1930s, research looked into the properties of the gel that is produced when a leaf is broken, and a chemical was found that stimulates the immune system. However, aloe vera is most commonly known to soothe burns – the gel forms a protective seal over the wound and helps the skin to heal beneath it. It is also beneficial for fungal infections such as ringworm, as well as minor cases of sunburn and eczema.

Pot marigold petals are antiseptic, while the plant's other healing properties help to prevent the spread of infection. A cream made from the petals also makes an excellent remedy for sore or inflamed skin.

Oil made from the flowers of St John's wort can be applied to nerve-damaged skin in conditions such as shingles, rashes and minor burns, to help it regenerate. Don't use it too often, though, as excessive use can cause the skin to become very sensitive to light and make it prone to sunburn.

TIP Keep an aloe vera plant in the kitchen, so whenever you burn yourself you can break off a piece of leaf and apply the gel to the wound.

Make a lavender bath bag

Soothe the skin

Swift spring onions, page 110

Salad

Tasty winter salads

There's nothing like the taste of home-grown salads, and even when summer's over, you can still enjoy fresh pickings.

Time to sow: early autumn

Sow a selection of lettuce and salad leaves in early autumn and you'll be harvesting from late autumn until spring. The earlier you sow, the sooner you'll be picking, so don't delay. For best results, sowings should be completed by mid- to late September.

Although the range of lettuce and salad leaf varieties for early autumn sowing isn't as wide as it is for spring sowing, most seed companies do offer a good selection. When choosing varieties, select hardy types, as they'll cope with the harsh winter conditions. Many summer salads simply won't tolerate the cold and wet of a typical winter outside.

There are two ways you can grow winter salads. The first is simply to sow the seeds directly outside. The second is to raise young plants in pots or modules, then plant them out later. Whichever method you choose, remember to pick a warm, sheltered site. Light and warmth are crucial for successful winter salad crops, and the protection of a cloche is vital through the winter months.

TIP Good salad crops to sow in early autumn include cut-and-come-again varieties of lettuce, wild rocket, mizuna and corn salad (sometimes sold as lamb's lettuce).

Grow watercress

You don't need a stream or a pond to grow watercress successfully. It's easy to raise from seed and will provide crops of delicious leaves all summer.

Time to sow: spring–autumn

Sowing watercress is simple – it will easily germinate in pots, just like mustard and cress. Either raise indoors or sow direct outside, in a shady place, from late spring to early autumn.

To sow indoors, fill some small pots with compost, sprinkle the seeds over the surface and water well. Seeds germinate readily in a couple of weeks. Keep watered and place in good light.

Once the seedlings have developed good root systems, split them into small clumps and transplant into larger pots. Water regularly and check the pots to make sure they're kept moist at all times. In 4–6 weeks, the watercress will be ready to harvest.

Regular harvesting will encourage the plants to keep producing fresh leaves. These spicy-tasting leaves are packed with calcium and iron, making them a great addition to a healthy diet.

TIP A good variety to try is 'Aqua', which is available from mail-order seed companies.

Tasty winter salads

Grow watercress

Super salads and leaves

Sow leafy vegetables that will crop all summer long.

Time to sow: spring–summer

Cut-and-come-again salad crops are great for picking regularly, a few leaves at a time. Spinach, mustards, many lettuces and chard are the best for frequent picking, producing tender new leaves every couple of days in summer. The brilliantly coloured stems and crinkled leaves of chard are great for adding to salads when young, and for steaming if they are left to mature.

Chard is very quick and easy to germinate and should be sown in spring for summer harvesting, and then again in midsummer for a later crop. Good varieties of chard include 'Bright Lights', which has yellow, red, pink and white stems with large leaves; 'Ruby Chard' or 'Rhubarb Chard', has bright red stems and finer leaves.

TIP Overwinter your summer sowing of chard under fleece for early pickings the following spring.

Quick and tasty mini leaves

Cress and other microgreens take up little space and grow in no time at all.

Time to sow: all year

Different cresses and microgreens will add interest and flavour to your salads and sandwiches. Growing cress is something most of us have done as a child, usually sprouting the conventional 'mustard and cress' on trays of damp kitchen paper.

These days, chefs have embraced the idea of tender, tasty sprouting seeds, and now seed companies offer a range of other options to try. All are designed to be eaten as young seedlings, often 6–15 days after sowing, before their 'true leaves' appear. Many of these microgreens are highly nutritious. Broccoli cress is easy, colourful, and very good for you, while tiny coriander leaves, fennel shoots and radish shoots are fabulous additions to salads and make attractive garnishes for cooked dishes.

Seeds can be sown directly into beds or containers outdoors in late spring and summer, and harvested when young, but for best results sow indoors all year round. Fill pots or seed trays with vermiculite, not compost, and scatter the seeds thinly over the surface. Place the pots on the kitchen windowsill or in the greenhouse to germinate.

TIP Experiment with different flavours – onions, red cabbage and pea shoots are also very good.

Quick and tasty mini leaves

Super salads and leaves

Start salads in guttering

Trying out new ways to sow and grow crops is not only fun, but also can lead to greater success than more conventional methods.

Time to sow: spring

Sowing salads in guttering indoors and then transplanting them outside produces more reliable results than sowing outdoors. All you need to do is cut a length of plastic guttering into short sections and fill each one with peat-free compost, stopping just short of the ends. Firm it down gently, so that it's level with the rim.

Space the seeds evenly along the length of the guttering, in rows. Keep them in an unheated greenhouse and the seeds should germinate in about a week.

When the seedlings are ready to plant out, dig a shallow trench across your vegetable beds to the depth of your guttering. Test it for size with the piece of guttering, without removing the plants. Once the site is prepared, gently slide the whole row of salad plants and compost straight out of the guttering and into the trench. Break it into shorter sections if this is easier.

Water the salads really well to settle their roots into their new home.

TIP This technique also works brilliantly with peas.

Try sprouting seeds

Most people think of bean sprouts as the long, white mung bean sprouts traditionally used in Chinese cooking. But there is a wide range of sprouting seeds, including sunflower, onion and basil, each with their own distinct flavour.

Time to sow: any time of year

Sprouting seeds are delicious raw in salads or cooked in stir-fries, and are highly nutritious. Best of all, they're extremely easy to grow. All you need is a jam jar, water and a piece of muslin, and the seeds are ready to eat in about a week. You can buy the seeds at the garden centre or by mail order.

To sprout the seeds, put a handful of seeds in a jar and cover well with water. Place a piece of muslin over the top of the jar and leave the seeds to soak overnight. The next morning, drain the water out through the muslin, rinse the seeds in fresh water and drain again, then place the jar on its side. Rinse the seeds at least twice daily through the muslin cloth until the sprouts are ready to eat. Rinse the sprouts again before eating.

Good seeds to try include: lentil sprouts – a member of the pea family, they have a nutty flavour; the colourful shoots of beet, which are perfect for salads and have a delicate beetroot taste; spring onions, which have a mild onion flavour that makes them ideal for salads or sandwiches.

TIP A good kids' gardening project is to get them sprouting alfalfa seeds. They are among the fastest to grow, and the sprouts are usually ready within 2–4 days.

Start salads in guttering

Try sprouting seeds

Early salads under cover

Supermarkets sell a wide range of salad leaves, but you'll find that few are organically grown and they are often not as fresh as they might be, so it is far better to grow your own.

Time to plant: late winter–early spring

Provided light levels are high enough, it is worth growing a few lettuces or salad-leaf plants in your greenhouse in late winter and early spring or under a mini-tunnel made of polythene or fleece, bought at any garden centre.

If your greenhouse has soil-filled borders, grow salad leaves before crops such as tomatoes are planted, then later you can fit them in among the crops. Cover salad plants to encourage rapid growth and earlier cropping. You could use fleece or mini-cloches, but individual bell cloches seem to work best. Choose ones with a vent in the top, so there is good air circulation.

Covering plants also helps to protect them from slugs and snails, which find the succulent young leaves as irresistible as we do.

TIP There's a great selection of salad seeds available, including special mixtures. However, if you have favourite types of salad, it's worth buying individual packets and combining them in your own mix.

Ripen the last tomatoes

If the last tomato fruits are still hanging off your plants in autumn, with light and temperature levels falling, it's time to give nature a helping hand.

Time to do: early–mid-autumn

If you are happy to maintain plants a little longer, any extra weather protection you can give will help, so around mid-autumn lay outdoor tomato plants gently on to a thick mat of straw and cover them with a cloche. Any miserable, drawn plants that you have left are ready for the compost heap.

Rather than waste the remaining fruits, pick them off and place them in a paper bag with an overripe banana – choose the freckled and squidgy sort left in the bottom of the fruit bowl. The ethylene gas given off by this banana acts as a natural ripening agent and turns green tomatoes red. The end result is probably a lot more appealing than yet another batch of green tomato chutney.

TIP You can still rescue and lay down tomato plants well into the autumn by covering them with a layer or two of loosely draped fleece.

Ripen the last tomatoes

Early salads under cover

Grow rocket from seed

Rocket has shot up fast in the trendy-eating stakes – everyone seems to love its spicy, almost peppery flavour. Better still, it is very easy to grow.

Time to sow: early spring–early autumn

A single packet of seeds is usually enough to sow a row 3–6m (10–20ft) long, depending on the variety of rocket you choose. There are always plenty of seeds in a packet. Ideally, use just a small quantity at one go.

Sow a pinch of seeds every few weeks and as each plant finishes another will be ready for cropping. That way you will be able to harvest the delicious leaves over a longer period.

The only real problem you'll have with rocket is the flea beetle, which eats the leaves, biting out tiny circular holes. If you sow seed in summer, the flea beetle will be particularly troublesome. The simple solution is to cover the row with a length of horticultural fleece or a fleece-covered mini-tunnel. You should get a perfect-looking and fine-tasting harvest within weeks.

TIP Rocket is best sown from early spring to early autumn, but later sowings will reward you with a good crop of surprisingly tender leaves.

Swift spring onions

Get bumper crops from a small space by repeat-sowing spring onions.

Time to sow: spring–late summer

Spring onions make a marvellous crop for the small-space gardener, as they can be planted close together and repeat-sown throughout the season. They are delicious in stir-fries and salads.

Seeds sown in late summer will overwinter to provide early pickings in spring, and even the thinnings can be snipped like chives and added to salads.

Spring onions are actually immature 'true' onions and need to be sown close together to prevent the bulbs developing. Sow them every couple of weeks from late winter through to late summer, in between slower-growing crops, for a continuous supply. Sow in drills 1cm (½in) deep in rows 10cm (4in) apart and water the drills before sowing if the soil is dry.

Good varieties include 'White Lisbon', which is tasty and quick growing; 'Winter White Bunching', a reliable overwintering variety.

TIP Water well in dry weather, especially before harvesting as it makes pulling the plants easier.

Keep sowing lettuces

Sow lettuces little and often for salad all summer long.

Time to sow: spring–mid-summer

Lettuces need very little space to grow quickly and crop consistently. The downside is that they tend to be ready all at once, and before you know it they're past their best. So, to keep a steady crop coming, it's best to sow a few seeds at a time and repeat-sow every couple of weeks through the summer months.

This successional sowing is perfect for lettuce varieties where the whole head is harvested, rather than the cut-and-come-again types that should keep going all season long.

Sow a short row of seeds and thin to the correct spacing, or sow seeds into modules and plant out when they're large enough. Repeat-sow 2–3 weeks later, and again 2–3 weeks after that. Stop sowing in late summer, as after that the plants may not have time to develop fully.

Good varieties include 'Little Gem Pearl', which is ideal for small spaces; 'Buttercrunch', which is a butterhead type; 'Pandero', with deep red leaves.

TIP Water the plants regularly, otherwise the leaves will become bitter.

Compost bags as growing bags

Even gardeners with lots of open ground often opt to raise their tomatoes in grow bags, but it can be more effective to use bags of compost instead.

Growing bags can work well, although keeping plants adequately moist can be quite a challenge, because the volume of compost is relatively small, and it can be hard to re-wet if allowed to dry out. To get around this problem, use a bag of regular compost instead; the larger volume of compost makes life a lot easier.

Plant out your tomatoes into a bag when they are about 15cm (6in) high. Water the plants in their pots half an hour before you transplant them. Shake the bag to break up any large clumps of compost and, using a sharp knife, remove a rectangle of plastic from one face of the bag. Fluff up the compost further with a hand fork or trowel, then dig the first planting hole, making it a bit larger than the plant pot.

Ease the plant from its pot. Cradle its rootball, supporting the plant's stem with your fingers. Place the young plant in its hole with the rootball just beneath the compost's surface and firm it in. Repeat, putting three plants in each bag. Stab small holes in the base for drainage, then water well.

TIP Buy a good-quality compost for your tomatoes, but whatever you buy will usually be better quality than many growing bags available.

When to harvest

The high water content of most salads means that in hot weather you'll notice a difference in the succulence of your salads according to the time of day they are picked. So when is the best time to harvest?

Time to do: late spring–autumn

Salad crops are best picked in the early morning, before they experience the dehydrating effects of the sun. Alternatively, give the plants a thorough drenching and then harvest them a few hours later, once they've had a chance to absorb the water.

However, you will get the strongest flavour from tomatoes if they are harvested before watering, because water is absorbed quickly by the plant and a recent drenching will reduce the intensity of the tomatoes' flavour.

Bear in mind, too, when harvesting salads, that younger leaves tend to be crisper and tastier than older ones. Plants with heads of leaves, such as lettuces, are best if the older, outer leaves are removed, leaving only the young, tasty ones.

TIP Don't store damaged crops, as they will not last as long as perfect ones. Instead use them as soon as you've picked them, eating them raw or cooking them in a sauce.

Super-speedy crops

Keep your crops coming throughout the season by sowing fast-maturing vegetables.

Time to sow: spring–summer

Quick-growing crops add variety to your meals in the summer months. A handful of radishes needs very little space and takes no time to grow – they can be ready to harvest in as little as 5 weeks.

Keep sowing small amounts of fast-maturing vegetables, such as radishes and spring onions, to supplement the steady crops from beans, peas and cut-and-come-again lettuces. Such crops will fill any gaps in the vegetable patch; you can even grow small crops in pots and window boxes.

Good varieties include radish 'Cherry Belle', which is round and bright red; spring onion 'White Lisbon', a fast-maturing favourite.

TIP Sow spring onions and lettuces in late summer for an early harvest the following spring.

Super-speedy crops

When to harvest

Success with beans, page 132

Vegetables

Keep leeks healthy

The key to keeping leeks healthy starts from the first sowings. While in most areas you can sow leeks outdoors in early or mid-spring, it's best to sow them in pots or trays at this time, as this seems dramatically to reduce the number of pest and disease casualties in those first weeks.

Time to sow: early–mid-spring

Sow leek seeds thinly so that the tiny grass-like seedlings can later be transplanted into fresh compost in a larger pot, where they will rapidly increase in size. By early summer they should be ready for planting out in the garden.

Leeks are not a particularly fussy crop and will do well in most soils, especially well-manured, heavy ones. The only problem you are likely to encounter is fungal rust, to which they are very prone – this is visible as orange or brown marks which cover the leaves and stems.

Rust-resistant, or at least tolerant, varieties are the best leeks to grow, as there is no chemical control available to gardeners. Good ones to try include 'Neptune', 'Autumn Mammoth 2' and 'Alvito'. However, don't be surprised if some rust does appear, especially if late summer and early autumn is rather wet.

TIP Never put infected plants on the compost heap. If you do, the problem will carry over to the next year, because the fungal spores will remain in the compost.

Bigger, better onions

Onions are particularly vulnerable to competition from weeds. That's because onion plants provide very little leaf cover to shade the ground around them and prevent weeds sprouting. But there are ways to defend your onions and beat the weeds.

Time to do: spring–summer

A well-nourished soil will provide perfect conditions for weeds, as well as for your crops, and can mean they grow extremely fast and cause a lot of competition.

Regular weeding is essential to produce healthy crops. If you let weeds get established, they will certainly reduce air circulation around onion plants. However, removing well-established weeds is more likely to disturb the onions, so it's probably best just to hoe off the tops.

Weeding by hand around onions and garlic works well, as you can pull out any deep-rooted perennials and hoe off any sprouting annual weeds. On a hot day you could leave annual weeds on the soil surface to dry up and die, but otherwise put them on the compost heap. It is important to remove the old weeds in order to avoid increasing the moisture levels in the air, which can lead to downy mildew disease.

TIP An onion hoe is perfect for hoeing off weeds – its small head fits neatly between the rows of swelling bulbs, and it's easy to manoeuvre without damaging the crops.

Keep leeks healthy

Bigger, better onions

Move your crops around

Sowing one type of crop into the same patch of soil again and again will cause a build-up of pests and diseases. Having attracted the pest or disease in one year, by replanting the same crop you are providing it again with host plants on which it will thrive. Instead, you need to change the crop, so the pests and diseases die out.

Many problems with crops can be avoided if you move different vegetables from one place to another each year. Different types of crop require varying amounts of nutrients. By swapping the main groups of vegetables around in a regular order, you can make the most efficient use of the nutrients in the soil. Anyone wanting to grow veg using minimal fertiliser should use this system. Divide your crops into four main groups: root crops, potato family (including tomatoes), brassicas (cabbage family), and legumes (peas and beans). Each group of crops is prone to similar problems, so moving them around helps to stop these diseases building up. Draw your veg plot and each bed in a notebook, and mark up where you will plant particular crops. Make sure each of the four groups only grows in the same spot once every four years. This means rotating the crops from bed to bed or area to area every spring.

TIP **If you have four veg beds, reserve one for roots, one for legumes, one for brassicas and one for potatoes.**

Keep cropping for longer

Late summer is the time of year when so many of the plants you have grown and nurtured are filling your plate, and maybe your freezer too. However, although your trug may be full, this is not a time to rest on your laurels. There are several simple ways to keep fruit and vegetables cropping for as long as possible.

Time to do: late summer

If the weather is dry, regular watering will help to prolong crops, but in late summer it is even more important to avoid wetting the plants' foliage, as diseases such as mildew and rust thrive in damp conditions.

Plants such as tomatoes, aubergines and peppers will carry on producing useful harvests if given a bit of protection from cooler temperatures.

To keep temperatures around plants a little higher, use horticultural fleece held in place with ground pegs or bricks, or mini fleece tunnels. Alternatively, old net curtains work just as well – they are both strong and economical. For individual plants, sturdy clear-plastic bell cloches are a great solution.

TIP **Whenever possible, pick crops and eat them straight away. Harvesting little and often means everything is in peak condition and packed full of flavour, juice and vitamins.**

Keep cropping for longer

Move your crops around

Enjoy the sweetest corn

Freshly picked sweetcorn is a real treat in late summer, but however much you love it, try to restrain yourself and grow only one variety. Having more than one risks cross-pollination, which results in a less sweet crop.

Time to plant: late spring–early summer

The breeders have been busy when it comes to sweetcorn and you'll find a great selection of different varieties in seed catalogues. Look for ones that have been bred to produce reliable results in our less than reliable climate, such as 'Conqueror'.

When planting, arrange plants in a block instead of rows. This will help to increase the rate of successful pollination for this wind-pollinated crop, even if you only have a few plants.

As soon as the golden tassels are starting to turn brown, the cobs are ready to harvest. Leave them on too long and the kernels will become tougher and starchier. Cook the cobs immediately after harvesting, because the moment they leave the plant the sugars in the kernels start converting into starches.

TIP If you can't resist growing more than one variety of sweetcorn, make sure you pick 'tendersweet' ones, such as 'Lark', as these don't need to be isolated from other varieties.

Fuss-free leeks

A lot of people seem to shy away from growing leeks – perhaps they are too closely associated with horticultural shows rather than good eating? Yet this is an easy crop and a great way to provide vegetables at a less productive time of year.

Time to plant: spring

The traditional technique of 'earthing up' leeks can put people off – but it's actually very easy. All you do is plant the leeks quite shallowly, about 8cm (3in), in a pencil-thick hole that you fill up with water, not earth. Then, three or more times during the growing season you simply draw up the soil around the stems, about 5cm (2in) each time.

By early to mid-autumn, the first leeks are ready for lifting. Loosen the soil beneath the plant with a fork, then they are easily harvested by hand. Soil still clinging to the base can be shaken back on to the bed or added to the compost bin, together with the outer leaves.

Mid- to late-cropping varieties are particularly hardy, and some can safely be left in the soil throughout winter.

TIP Earthing up produces well-blanched stems, but it is quite time-consuming. To avoid the bother, simply plant them deeper, to about 15–20cm (6–8in). This makes leeks a truly easy, trouble-free crop.

Enjoy the sweetest corn

Fuss-free leeks

Try mangetout peas

The word mangetout translates literally as 'eat all', and that is precisely what you can do with this delicious pea. Forget fiddly shelling – with mangetouts you can eat the tender pod as well as the developing peas within, so they are well worth a spot in your veg garden.

Time to sow: spring–early summer

Mangetouts thrive in a sunny spot on a neutral to alkaline soil – preferably one that has had plenty of organic matter incorporated during the previous winter.

Seed catalogues contain mouth-watering descriptions of mangetout varieties. Favourites are 'Oregon Sugar Pod', 'Delikata' and 'Sugar Snap'. The latter two are suitable for eating as mangetouts, or you can leave the pods on the plants to develop fully, then shell them like normal peas.

Sow the seed from early spring until early summer. Remember to harvest crops regularly, because edible peas, much like their ornamental relative the sweet pea, will soon slow down and cease to crop prolifically if they are not promptly picked.

Harvest when the pods are 8cm (3in) or less in length and they will melt in your mouth.

TIP Mangetouts are delicious lightly cooked and simply drenched in butter or tossed in a salad or stir-fry. If eaten shortly after harvesting, they beat any other peas you can ever buy in the shops.

Colourful carrots

Growing your own carrots can be a real eye-opener. You'll be amazed at the fantastically sweet, strong flavour of some varieties. What's more, they're now available in a startling array of colours (although sometimes at the expense of flavour and texture).

Time to sow: early spring–midsummer

Choose your carrot variety carefully and you'll get that satisfying feeling of pulling your own carrots and, just minutes later, finding out what a carrot should really taste like.

'Purple Dragon' is one of the best of the colourful varieties. To say it is extraordinary to look at would be an understatement. With its really strong, dark purple skin, it's such a surprise to find the tempting orange flesh within. The texture and flavour make it an absolute pleasure to eat raw, steamed or in a stir-fry.

'Kinbi' is one of the best of the paler colours. It has an extremely pretty yellow root – much brighter yellow than most – that would add interest to any salad. It has a slightly stumpy shape and a better flavour than other varieties without orange flesh.

TIP If you can, try before you buy and don't fall for a carrot because of its unusual colour – there is a white variety called 'Belgian White', but it is rather lacking in flavour.

Try mangetout peas

Colourful carrots

Veg in the flower beds

You don't need a huge garden to grow your own veg – they grow equally well mixed in with the flowers in a border as they do in their own separate space.

Time to plant: spring

There's no reason why your border can't look as delicious as it tastes. A bed where the crops are harvested regularly, when they are small and tasty, allows you to space plants more closely than generally recommended, so you can squeeze a surprising amount in. Good plants for such a bed include lettuce and beetroot. If your borders need some height and a focal point, include wigwams of climbing beans (see p46) or towering sweetcorn or artichokes, in bigger borders.

For the best results, plant your edible border in the sunniest spot you can find in the garden and prepare the ground carefully. This will help to ensure good growth and encourage your crops to ripen well.

Keep the border well watered, especially in its early stages and during any prolonged dry spells, and particularly if your soil is stony and free-draining.

Watch out for garden pests such as greenfly, caterpillars and slugs, and deal with them swiftly before they make inroads into your crop.

TIP A veg and ornamental border should fill out within 8 weeks of planting. Of course, some crops mature faster than others, but by sowing a pinch of seed every few weeks you can replace those already harvested.

Keeping warm in winter

Wrap up your soil in winter and you'll be rewarded in spring with warmer, more workable ground.

Carpet and black plastic are both excellent ways to cover bare ground during winter. First, they stop any weeds growing, and it's staggering how many will grow, even in the depths of winter. Second, they keep the soil warm and workable, allowing you simply to lift them off an area and dig it over in frosty weather when others can't touch their plot. It's best to avoid working the soil when frozen, as you destroy its structure.

Cast-off hessian-backed stair carpets are perfect as they can be laid in lengths, unlike a huge square piece from a room. Foam-backed, nylon carpets are awful, as they disintegrate, leaving bits all over your vegetable plot.

Alternatively, use flattened cardboard boxes weighted down with stones and bricks, or black plastic sheeting with slits to allow rain through. It has to be black to absorb warmth from the sun. But it's better to invest in some woven ground-cover material from the garden centre, because it's porous and lasts for ages. Buy it off the roll rather than pre-packed, as it tends to be cheaper that way.

Feeding know-how

Confused about what, when and how to feed your veg? Don't worry – it's not as difficult as it seems, and there are several easy methods that will stop your plants going hungry.

Time to act: autumn, winter and summer

You'll go a long way to maintaining the fertility and structure of your soil by simply covering the ground with an 8–10cm (3–4in) deep layer of organic matter, such as well-rotted manure, each year. Spread it on the soil in autumn and the worms will work it into the ground over the winter.

This is particularly beneficial on light soils where heavy winter rainfall can cause nutrients to be washed out. Any organic matter remaining on the surface in spring can then be simply forked in.

Manure is as much as most plants require, as over-feeding can produce soft, floppy growth. Pelleted chicken manure is useful as a fertiliser, but check it is from an organic source if your plot is organic. The pellets can be incorporated with a good degree of accuracy and have a noticeable effect on the plants. Spring is the best time to apply it to most crops.

Fruiting plants benefit from feeding with a fertiliser high in potash, such as tomato food.

TIP Where quick results are required, fertiliser will be taken up faster by the plants if it is applied as a liquid feed to the roots, or sprayed on the leaves.

Try something different

If you're a fan of broccoli, then you should try some of the tasty purple-sprouting varieties for a really tender, tasty vegetable in winter and spring. Sow broccoli seeds in mid- to late spring into a seed bed of well-dug and well-raked soil.

Time to sow: mid–late spring

Keep the area clear of weeds and thin the seedlings to about 8cm (3in) apart for sturdy plants. It is important to keep the weeds down, as they will compete with your crop and large weeds will shade the seedlings, making them weaker, more spindly and more prone to disease.

When the seedlings are about 8cm (3in) high with five or six leaves, they can be transferred from the seed bed to their final positions. Check the seed packet of the variety you choose, but it is usually best to leave about 60cm (2ft) between the plants.

There are plenty of excellent varieties available, including 'Rudolph', which produces rich purple spears from around Christmas time. Another good one to try is 'Claret', which is an F1 hybrid with wine-red spears that crops heavily from mid- to late spring.

TIP Always keep a few seeds spare in case there are any disasters with seedlings, such as an early slug attack or a trampling child.

Make a wigwam

Good, robust wigwams are a brilliant addition to any vegetable patch and are perfect for supporting a range of climbing crops, including beans and pumpkins.

To ensure that the structure doesn't blow away, you need the verticals of your wigwam to sink a good 15–20cm (6–8in) into the ground. It should then stand at least 2m (6ft), or even better 2.1m (7ft), up in the air. Once any bean, sweet pea or nasturtium is growing at full tilt it will swamp anything smaller.

You can buy big wigwams from a good willow supplier, or you can make your own. You will need at least eight straight sticks, such as hazel or silver birch, or bamboo canes, along with tarred string, Flexi-Ties or coated wire.

Draw a circle about 1m (40in) in diameter in the soil with a stick. Poke one of your uprights in, then another about 30cm (12in) away, then the next, and so on. You'll then have a circle of wooden uprights. Gather them up at the top and tie them together with thestring, Flexi-Tie or coated wire.

TIP Make sure the wigwam is high enough for your purposes – to make them easy to put on the roof of a car, most frames available at garden centres are far too small.

Outdoor aubergines

Aubergines need plenty of bright sunshine to do well, far more than crops such as tomatoes and sweet peppers, so you need to plant them where they can bask in maximum sunlight.

Time to plant: early summer

Aubergines enjoying growing in a greenhouse, but don't despair if you don't have one as they are happy outside too, as long as they're given a bit of extra protection, such as polythene covers. A great advantage with plants that are grown outside is that they don't tend to suffer from whitefly, a pest that can get to plague-like proportions in a greenhouse.

You'll find plenty of young aubergine plants at garden centres in late spring, ready to plant outside after last frosts. Put them into large pots or grow bags for harvesting from late summer onwards. Towards late autumn the plants do need extra protection, but you can still collect fruits from plants grown under polythene covers after the first frosts.

Feed aubergine plants in the same way that you would tomatoes, using a high-potash liquid tomato fertiliser at half strength to encourage good flowers and fruit.

TIP Aubergines hate having their feet too wet, so keep their soil or compost just moist at all times.

Make a wigwam

Outdoor aubergines

Make space for courgettes

Picked when really young and tender, courgettes are excellent for cooking, stir-frying and adding to salads. Reckon on getting at least a dozen courgettes off a single plant, so they're a great use of space.

Time to sow: mid-spring

Courgettes are one of the easiest vegetables to grow. Like many crops, the more regularly you harvest them, the more fruits form.

Many people prefer the green-skinned varieties such as 'Defender' and 'Zucchini', because they're heavier croppers and their skins can be more tender than the yellow varieties such as 'Gold Rush' and 'Taxi'.

If you like experimenting with different varieties, try a few of the spherical courgettes such as 'Leprechaun' as well. Harvest these when they are very tender, slightly larger than a tennis ball. Slice the top off, scoop out some of the flesh and you have a courgette perfect for stuffing.

The huge bright yellow flowers of any type of courgette are also a real delicacy. In smart restaurants you occasionally find them lightly coated in batter and deep fried, or stuffed with ricotta cheese. Harvesting the flowers, still perky and intact, is easy when you grow your own.

TIP Courgettes are ready to pick as soon as they are anything upwards of the thickness of your thumb.

Get a taste for winter chicory

If you long for freshly picked leaves in your food in winter, perk up your dishes with some home-grown forced chicory, which is delicious when braised or sliced up in a salad.

Time to do: sow in June–July, force in Nov–Dec

Witloof chicory is the best type for forcing. Sow the seeds in June or July in rows 30cm (12in) apart, then leave them to grow. In around November, dig up the chicory plants, cut off the top growth, leaving 2.5cm (1in) of leaves, and trim the roots to 20cm (8in). Store the roots in dry compost in a cool shed or garage, where they will stay dormant until you need them.

Take three or four roots at a time, to stagger your crop, and plant them in pots of compost or garden soil. Bring them inside, cover them with a box, an upturned bin or anything else that will block out the light, just as you would with rhubarb, and place them in a warm, dark location. Water occasionally, and after a few weeks new buds should appear. Wait until these are 7.5–10cm (3-4in) tall (after three to four weeks), then cut them off at the base, eat and enjoy!

TIP Don't throw out the roots once you've harvested the leaves – each root should produce a few more shoots before you need to replace it with a fresh root from store.

Get a taste for winter chicory

Make space for courgettes

Make raised beds

Raised beds not only make a vegetable garden look neat and tidy but they offer a number of practical benefits too.

Time to do: any time

Raised beds are a real saving grace if your garden soil is poor, as they can be filled with imported topsoil or loam-based compost to provide better growing conditions. If you build the raised beds around 1.2m (4ft) wide, you can tend them from the sides and never need to walk on them, so you won't get problems with soil compaction. Leave 45cm (18in) between beds to allow wheelbarrow access.

Organic matter can easily be added by simply covering the soil with a thick layer of compost or well-rotted manure in autumn and letting the worms pull it into the soil over the winter.

The raised height of the beds also means that drainage is good – a relief when your garden soil is clay and often soggy. Gardeners with back problems will also appreciate the raised height as it cuts down on the amount of bending needed to reach the crops.

Beds are simple to make or you can buy ready-made modular systems. To keep costs down, you can always make them using recycled old timber, such as scaffolding boards.

TIP If you can, run the beds from north to south to give your crops even sunlight levels.

Easy onions

While onions can be raised from seed, it's much easier to grow them from little bulbs called 'sets', which can be bought from garden centres or are available via mail order.

Time to plant: early–mid-spring

Before planting sets, dig the soil over thoroughly, removing any weeds and large stones.

Onions look best in army-straight rows, so this is the time to get out your gardening line. If you do not own one already you could improvise by just tying a length of twine or string to two pieces of quite sturdy cane.

Simply ease each small onion into the soil so that the tips are left protruding. If you want large onions, space the sets about 10cm (4in) apart. But if you prefer smaller ones, space them about 6cm (2½in) apart.

For the next few weeks, cover the newly planted rows with netting. If the sets are left uncovered they are likely to be removed by inquisitive birds, whereas if they are covered until they have rooted, you should be able to keep them all in place.

TIP The main crop is usually planted in early to mid-spring, but you could try putting in a few in mid-autumn the following year for an early spring crop.

Make raised beds

Easy onions

Success with beans

The taste and texture of home-grown beans is second to none, especially climbing French beans. These are similar in taste to runner beans but seem to produce more reliable crops and have fewer problems with bees cutting their way into the back of the flowers.

Time to sow: spring

Raise beans in trays or pots under glass as this produces better results than sowing outdoors, minimises the risk of seeds failing to germinate when the weather suddenly turns very wet and cold, and also cuts down on slug damage.

Watch out for frosts – If one is forecast, protect plants with a cloche. Similarly, if a spell of very dry weather arrives, make sure the plants are kept well watered, especially those that have recently been planted out.

Climbing beans need support, and a wigwam of wooden poles or bamboo canes is a popular choice (see p46). Any supports need to be firmly tied together and pushed well into the ground; a sudden strong gust of wind can cause an inadequately secured support to topple, especially once it is carrying a heavy crop of foliage and beans.

TIP Steam or microwave purple or golden varieties to keep their colour after cooking.

Plant asparagus

Asparagus is a real gourmet treat, and home-grown spears are far superior to those in the shops. They're quite easy to grow and well worth the effort for their flavour.

Time to plant: early spring

Good varieties of asparagus include: 'Connover's Colossal', which has a superb flavour, and 'Backlim' and 'Franklim', which produce consistently high yields.

Plant one-year-old crowns in early spring, 45cm (18in) apart, into ground that is rich, well-drained and well-manured, and cover the crowns with several inches of soil. Don't cut the spears, let them grow into mature plants and when these turn dead and brown at the end of the autumn, cut the ferny leaves off at ground level and build up the soil around the crowns. The following year manure the bed well, but don't cut the spears. In the third year, crop the spears lightly for about 4 weeks, then from the fourth year onwards, crop from late spring until the middle of summer. Leave all buds that appear after this date to grow into ferns.

Asparagus plants make a slow start but the same crowns will then crop successfully for more than 20 years.

Although slugs can be tiresome, the only real pests are asparagus beetles. These cream, red and black pests have to be despatched by hand.

TIP Cook asparagus the day it's picked. Break off the tough ends and steam slender spears. With thicker spears, loosely tie them together and place upright in a deep pan of water so the stems boil and the tips steam above the water. Cover and cook for 5–10 minutes, depending on their thickness.

Beat blight

It might not be obvious at first glance, but tomatoes and potatoes are close cousins. Sadly, this also means that they both suffer from the devastating disease called blight.

Plants with blight will suddenly look like they have been frosted or suffered a severe blast of windburn, then the next day they look charred and that's it – the whole lot have to be ripped out and disposed of.

Tomato and potato plants affected by blight have to be treated with a fortnightly spray of fungicide to ensure the plants survive. This fungus easily transfers between the two crops and tends to hang around. Without the fungicide your whole carefully tended crop may collapse in just 2–3 days in late summer, when the weather is wet and mild.

If you prefer to avoid the use of chemicals, grow tomato plants inside where they're more protected. Earthing up potato plants also helps to protect the tubers. Remove any diseased growth as soon as you see it and never compost it.

TIP Some varieties have been bred to resist blight, such as tomato 'Ferline' and potato 'Sarpo Mira'.

Prevent carrot problems

Freshly pulled, given a rinse and crunched without delay is the best way to eat carrots, but the thought of ones that are tunnelled by maggots is very unappetising.

Time to sow: spring–summer

Carrot fly larvae can be a real problem and prevention is the only solution. There are resistant varieties available, such as 'Sytan' and 'Flyaway', which work well, but not everyone enjoys their flavour. Instead, it's best to grow classic varieties such as 'Amsterdam Forcing 3' and 'Nantes' under protection.

To do this, make a simple wooden frame about 60cm (2ft) high and staple horticultural fleece to the sides. Adult carrot flies are low flying, rarely getting more than 45cm (18in) above soil level, so this barrier keeps them off the developing crop and prevents them laying their eggs there. The result? No eggs, no maggots and no tunnelling.

It's also a good idea to sow carrot seeds sparingly to avoid having to thin out the resulting seedlings (see p188).

TIP Planting other strongly scented crops such as onions or garlic can help deter carrot flies from their prize.

Enjoy a late crop of peas

Freshly picked, home-grown peas are so irresistible that it's hard to get them into the kitchen without munching them as you harvest them. With this in mind, it's worth sowing a few late plants in midsummer to give you a fresh burst of cropping right into autumn.

Time to sow: midsummer

By autumn, pea plants sown earlier in the year will have long since finished producing anything useful, and will quite often have succumbed to an attack of mildew too.

Sowing peas direct into the soil as late as midsummer usually works better than earlier sowings. If it is a bad year for slugs, though, you may prefer to raise the plants in cells or modules. Plant them out while they are still small because these young plants always have a really good root system. Provided the compost is just slightly moist when you remove them from the cell, the roots hold together well and are unlikely to get damaged.

Using a trowel, dig a small hole for each plant then pop them all in and water the whole area thoroughly. Drive supports into the soil close to the plants as soon as they are transplanted in order to minimise disturbance. The plantlets soon start to cling on with their tendrils.

TIP Twiggy sticks make the most attractive supports for peas. You can buy them from garden centres or you can save some suitable, well-branched prunings of your own.

Make onions last

Years ago, everyone used to suggest speeding up the ripening process of onions by bending the foliage over at the neck. Few people do this now, believing that it is far better gently but firmly to lift each bulb slightly with a fork, so breaking the roots.

Time to do: midsummer

This gentle method works well as long you wait until the foliage is just starting to yellow naturally in midsummer. If the weather happens to be unusually wet when you want to harvest your onions, you can lift the bulbs when the leaves are still green. However, as soon as the foliage is definitely on the turn to yellow, remove the bulbs completely from the soil and leave them on their sides to dry off in the summer sunshine.

If there is any chance of more than a very brief shower, then transfer the onions to a sheltered spot. A cold frame is good, but anywhere will do as long as it is well ventilated, light and warm.

Once the onions are dry, they can be stored in net bags or old tights. Alternatively, plait the foliage together to make a traditional onion string (see p170).

TIP It is essential to get the more moist, root-end of the bulbs clear of the soil for them to dry rapidly and thoroughly, so always give them plenty of space when you lay them out.

Make onions last

Enjoy a late crop of peas

Plant shallots

Shallots are one of the earliest crops you can plant outside in the new year, and are well worth growing if you love tasty food as they have a delicious, slightly milder flavour than onions.

Time to do: February–March

Growing your own shallots couldn't be easier. In February or March, plant the small bulbs (or sets), which are available from mail-order suppliers and many garden centres, straight into prepared ground. Space them 15cm (6in) apart, in rows about 20cm (8in) apart, to give them room to grow and allow you to easily hoe out any weeds that grow between them.

Place each bulb with its tip hidden just below soil level. All you need to do now is keep them weed free and well watered in dry spells, and your crop of shallots will be ready to harvest in July or August, when the leaves turn yellow naturally. Lift the clumps with a fork, taking care not to damage the bulbs, and dry them off in the sun if you're going to store them.

TIP Before planting, trim off any dry, wispy tops to prevent birds using them to tug the shallots out of the ground, or cover them with netting until they get established.

Boost your tomato crop

As summer goes on and your tomatoes are thriving and flowering, make a few regular and timely tweaks to keep your plants on track for a bumper harvest.

Time to do: July–September

When plants start to bear fruit stake them before they collapse under the weight of their crop. Drive a bamboo cane into the soil next to the plant, taking care not to damage its roots, then tie the stems to the cane with twine in one or more places, depending on how much support is needed.

Mid-summer is the time to capitalise on the sunshine in order to ripen the fruit. Removing the vigorous sideshoots that develop between the side branches and the main stem is an important job, as you don't want the plant using up its energy on these leafy shoots – you want it to put all its efforts into producing tomatoes. The leafy shoots can also shade the developing fruit, hindering the ripening process. To remove a young shoot, simply grasp it at the base, close to the main stem, and bend it sharply downwards to give a clean break.

As temperatures rise, water your tomato plants on a daily basis if possible, and to keep them cropping give the plants regular doses of specialist tomato feed once you see the first tiny fruit.

TIP If you've left a bit behind when pinching out a sideshoot, don't leave it as it may die back and damage the main stem. Pinch out the stump, taking care not to harm the adjacent growth. For other tips on boosting your tomato crop, turn to page 151.

Planting shallots

Boost your tomato crop

Brassicas under attack

Pest attacks on brassicas can leave your cabbages, cauliflowers, Brussels sprouts and broccoli looking rather sad and can drastically reduce your eventual harvest. But there are simple ways in which you can reduce the risk of attack.

Time to do: spring–summer

Keep pests at bay by covering crops with fleece or fine-mesh netting. Support it with a series of wire hoops to create a tunnel over the plants. This allows them space to grow and prevents the covering from touching the leaves – thereby inadvertently allowing the pests a way in.

If plants are protected from the moment they are planted out, you can avoid the caterpillars of cabbage white butterflies. By covering them, you will not need to spray the pests and you can look forward to top-quality veg for your dinner plate.

Pigeons are also a real pain when it comes to brassicas, as they love to eat the young shoots and will shred plants to pieces, but they can also be discouraged by netting.

TIP Don't chuck out old CDs or used bits of tin foil, instead hang these and anything that sparkles and glints in the light above crops to scare off greedy birds.

Grow better spuds

Potatoes are pretty easy plants to grow, but they do fall victim to a few problems that can be reduced by spending a little time using the technique of 'earthing up'.

Time to do: spring

Earthing up spuds – basically covering the new shoots with a layer of turned earth to create a long mound – is essential when the young shoots are around 15–20cm (6–8in) high in spring. The main reason for doing this is to prevent frost damage, but it also reduces the chances of harvesting tubers with a green tinge – which are poisonous to eat. Some varieties grow tubers close to the surface, and regular earthing up reduces greening.

Tubers buried a little deeper also seem to be less likely to be infected quickly if potato blight strikes. This devastating disease often attacks in periods of warm, wet weather and can cause the whole crop to rot. The spores that cause the disease wash down into the soil from infected plants, so the extra soil between the tuber and the soil surface can help to prevent the crop getting ruined.

When the potato shoots have reached about 25cm (10in), use a rake or spade to flick the soil upward. Work your way along the row of potatoes, carefully covering the shoots to create a neat mound. Just a few weeks later, plenty of foliage will sprout up as the shoots push through the mound.

TIP Earthing up is a little extra work, but it pays off at harvest time when the crop is easier to lift and produces fewer damaged tubers.

Brassicas under attack

Grow better spuds

Rent an allotment

If you're frustrated by the lack of space in your own garden, or don't want to grow veg among your flowers, why not get your hands on some new ground by renting an allotment?

Your local council will tell you where the nearest allotments to you are. Prices vary considerably, but the rent shouldn't break the bank – they tend to start from around £6 a year, although in London you could pay up to £60.

Many councils include free clearing and rotavating of the plot in the price to help you get started, so it's worth asking.

When it comes to choosing your plot, it pays to find out if there is a site representative. They will be able to tell you where the best soil is, point out any frost pockets, and outline which areas are windswept. Steer clear of steep slopes unless you're prepared to terrace the site, and look out for a plot near a water tap – it will save you leg-work in summer. If you can, pick a plot close to well-tended areas. The last thing you want is someone else's weed seeds blowing into your plot, or roots creeping under the fence.

Most allotment rental periods run from autumn to autumn, so in areas of high demand, be sure to get your name on the waiting list by summer.

TIP For help with plots or tips on allotments, join the National Society of Allotment and Leisure Gardeners.

Get composting

A compost bin – or preferably two or three – is something most gardeners want, and indeed need. It's amazing how much compostable material even a small garden can produce.

Autumn clearing always produces compostable waste; everything from old potato plants and brassica foliage, to the odd courgette and bean plant that is past its useful life. Almost any vegetable waste can be composted. Avoid adding meat and cooked foods, however, as these can attract vermin, and never use perennial weeds such as dandelions or diseased material, as these may not be killed by the composting process.

Whether you have a large or small bin, the contents must be turned to aerate them and aid the decomposition. Make sure that everything is mixed in well so that all parts are subjected to the higher temperatures at the centre and so break down evenly.

Compost prepared in summer should be ready for use after about 3 months; 6 months in winter. It can then be dug into the soil to improve its structure or used as a mulch on the surface to hold moisture in the soil below.

TIP Don't bin kitchen peelings, put them in a worm bin where they can be converted into compost and liquid feed.

Get composting

Get an allotment

Grow your own lemons, page 158

In the greenhouse and under cover

Spring clean your greenhouse

After winter and before you start sowing the summer's seeds is the ideal time to give your greenhouse a good clean.

Time to do: early spring

Light levels begin to increase in spring, but it is still essential to maximise all light. To ensure that seedlings and young plants inside the greenhouse get as much sunlight as possible, give the glass a good spring clean, inside and out. Start on the inside – you'll be amazed at how much gunk you can clear. An old washing-up brush and some soapy water, combined with a good deal of elbow grease, works wonders.

Glazed edges and the frame also need a clean up, as they are particularly good at harbouring dirt. Crevices such as these may also hide some overwintering pests such as snails or red spider mites, so use a bristled brush to winkle them out.

In mild weather you may be able to put your plants outside while you clean, perhaps covering them with a couple of layers of horticultural fleece. If this seems a bit risky, simply cram them all together at one end while you tackle the other, then change them round.

TIP A washing-up brush is ideal for cleaning the outside of the greenhouse, but dislodge any grime in between panes of glass by inserting a thin, flexible plant label and wiggling it about a bit.

Prolong your peppers

Peppers grown in greenhouses or good-sized coldframes should still produce fruits in autumn. Like so many sun lovers, peppers may need much of the summer to get going, and it is essential that you keep on giving them TLC at this time.

Time to do: autumn

Even inside a greenhouse temperatures will be considerably lower in autumn, so getting the watering regime right can be tricky. Although peppers need a fair amount of moisture, they detest sogginess around their roots. If the compost gets too dry, however, the fruits are likely to develop black bases, which are a sign of blossom end rot, caused by erratic watering. It's a delicate balance.

A plentiful supply of high potash feed is definitely in order. It's best to use the same fertiliser that you give to your tomatoes, and dose them with this every week.

Light levels are lower and the days shorter in autumn, so if there is space on the greenhouse staging, move the peppers in their pots off the greenhouse floor.

TIP Moving a grow bag full of plants is likely to produce disastrous results, but slipping a rigid board under the full length of the bag makes the task much less risky.

Spring clean your greenhouse

Prolong your peppers

Cultivate cucumbers

Cucumbers are productive plants to grow in a greenhouse and from just one plant you can get upwards of 15 delicious fruits.

Time to sow: mid–late spring

As long as you keep cucumbers warm to start with, protect them from scorching with shading paint or netting in hot temperatures, and keep an eye on the watering, they are easy to grow. Fruits should be ready to harvest from midsummer.

It is often said that you cannot grow cucumbers and tomatoes together because they need different growing conditions, but in actual fact they will be quite happy together and should produce a good crop.

Remember that cucumbers don't like draughts while too much moisture around the base of the stems can cause foot and root rots.

Either sow seeds in mid-spring or buy plants in late spring. Plant them on a slightly raised mound of soil to prevent water sitting around the stem. You can also direct water straight to the roots by sinking a flowerpot into the soil alongside the plant and watering into it.

TIP Cucumbers are climbing plants so they need support as they grow. A piece of trellis is ideal, but canes, wire or twine will do just as well.

Don't frazzle in the heat

When temperatures are high, it is important to keep the greenhouse well ventilated. This reduces the heat and humidity and ensures a good flow of air around the plants.

Time to do: spring and summer

Keeping windows open and having plenty of vents mean that bees are able to fly in and out to pollinate the crops, and good air circulation will help keep diseases to a minimum.

An automatic vent is a great help if you're away from home during the day as it will open and close the window, depending on the temperature. Make sure your greenhouse has lots of windows that can be opened and add extra vents if necessary to keep things cool. You can buy easy-to-fit vent kits at good garden centres.

Damping down is a great way to reduce temperatures too. This simply means hosing down the greenhouse floor with cool water. Alternatively, use a watering can. It's best to do it every morning if you can.

If you have them, pull down greenhouse blinds on hotter days, or try adding temporary shading paint to the glass to protect your plants from the sun's scorching summer rays.

TIP Don't forget that simply opening the door on a hot day is one of the best ways of allowing fresh air to get in and around the greenhouse.

Don't frazzle in the heat

Cultivate cucumbers

Juicy peaches

Peaches are one of the most delicious summer fruits but are often thought too exotic to grow in Britain. In fact, they are totally hardy.

Time to plant: late autumn and early spring

Although they can be grown outside in a sheltered position, peaches will crop more reliably in a greenhouse. A cold greenhouse will offer just enough protection from frost in early spring when the blossom is produced and will also stop the fungus that causes peach leaf curl from attacking the plant. This disease appears as red blisters on leaves that soon drop off. Infected plants should be sprayed with Bordeaux mixture and all affected leaves cleared away and disposed of carefully.

The easiest way to grow peaches is in a fan shape, either on a wall or at the end of a greenhouse. The size of the fan will depend on space, but an established plant that is 1.8m (6ft) wide will produce a crop of around 40 peaches.

TIP Try 'Peregrine', with white flesh; 'Rochester', a reliable cropper; and 'Duke of York', which has an intense flavour.

Baskets of early strawberries

One of the advantages of a greenhouse is that you can plant crops such as strawberries sooner than if they were outside, and with just a little heat you can be picking plump, juicy, red fruits a couple of weeks earlier.

Time to plant: spring

If space is at a premium in your greenhouse, why not grow your strawberries in a hanging basket? The natural trailing habit of strawberries makes them ideal for baskets and containers as they tumble over the sides.

You can use any type of basket, as long as it provides a good depth of compost, so that it doesn't dry out too quickly. Add water-retaining crystals to the compost further to reduce the amount of watering needed.

Plants are readily available at garden centres and via mail order from specialist fruit nurseries. Three plants should be about right for a 30–35cm (12–14in) basket. Keep the compost moist at all times and ply with tomato feed and you'll be enjoying fruits before the tennis at Wimbledon.

TIP Good early-fruiting strawberry varieties are 'Honeoye', 'Elvira' and 'Rosie'.

Juicy peaches

Baskets of early strawberries

Turn up the heat

In early spring a heated propagator is always in demand, even if you keep the greenhouse frost free. The extra heat they offer hugely increases the range of crops you can start off yourself, and means you can get them up and running earlier.

Time to do: late winter–early spring

You can sow seed in trays or modular trays, or simply use an ordinary flowerpot in your propagator.

Crops suitable for raising in a heated propagator include chilli peppers, sweet peppers, asparagus, melons, aubergines, greenhouse cucumbers, marrows, tomatoes, courgettes, broccoli and herbs such as basil.

Peppers and greenhouse tomatoes will really benefit from a heated propagator and should produce a greater crop because the plants will be ready that bit earlier in the year.

For maximum efficiency, keep the propagator in a relatively warm, or at least protected, position. Most entry-level models raise the heat inside the propagator to a fixed point – often 10–20°C – above surrounding air temperature. A propagator that allows you to regulate the heat will make life easier, but by simply raising the seed tray or pot off the base of the propagator you can germinate seeds that require a lower temperature.

TIP To reduce heating costs, make sure the compost is not freezing cold when you sow seed.

Hassle-free watering

When the weather is warm, greenhouse plants need watering at least once a day, but this needn't be a hassle if you install an irrigation system to do it for you.

Time to do: spring–summer

There is a good selection of irrigation systems available, ranging from simple capillary benches to full-blown watering systems controlled by an electronic timer.

A battery-operated timer can be programmed to water several times a day for a set period. Timers can be attached to sprinklers, irrigation systems or soaker hoses.

A dripper system can be the best solution when there are lots of different plants spread around the greenhouse. A kit comes with drippers, sprinklers and clips. Once set up, simply adjust the flow of water according to the weather conditions.

To water hanging baskets, containers or grow bags, a simple dripper system can be run from a large water-filled bag. A short length of tube will slowly deliver the water to your plants.

TIP Install an irrigation system before you go away on holiday and you can leave the greenhouse to look after itself rather than having to ask friends and neighbours to pop in and water.

Get better tomatoes

Tomatoes generally thrive in a warm greenhouse when adequately looked after, but there are also a few tricks of the trade to help produce an even better crop.

Time to do: late spring–early summer

Tomatoes grow best in the greenhouse border, which provides them with a good volume of soil. This makes watering easier, too, because they need watering less often than plants grown in containers or grow bags.

Even in a well-manured border, it's best to provide supplementary feeding because tomatoes thrive on it. Potash, in particular, will help to keep the plants cropping well, and liquid fertilisers specially formulated for tomatoes prove invaluable. The rate and frequency at which these need to be applied varies, so always check the label carefully.

TIP Tomatoes also benefit from regular removal of the sideshoots. For more information on how to do this, turn to page 136.

Success with seeds

Spring is the perfect time to sow many vegetable seeds in pots or trays inside, especially tender crops such as courgettes, which will need to be raised and grown on outside.

Time to sow: spring

Whatever container you use, make sure it is well scrubbed out before you start, so you don't introduce damping-off disease. This common problem causes young seedlings suddenly to collapse and die. Good hygiene is essential to prevent it, and an occasional watering with Cheshunt compound will also help.

Cell or module trays are especially useful for sowing vegetable seeds as they will keep pricking out and transplanting to a minimum.

Sow two seeds per cell as an insurance policy – if both seeds germinate, you can simply weed out the less vigorous seedling early on.

There are many different types of compost available and what you use is up to you, but generally one designed for seed sowing will produce the best results.

TIP In these days of water shortages, avoid using water from a butt for seedlings. Damping off can be kept at bay by using mains water.

Try biological pest controls

If you're not keen on using chemicals to treat pests and diseases on your fruit and veg, biological controls could be the answer to your problems.

Biological controls work by introducing a large number of natural predators into the greenhouse to attack pests on affected plants. Provided you have suitable conditions, such as adequate temperatures and freedom from any pesticides, these controls really do work.

Some common predators are the parasitic wasp *Encarsia formosa*, used against whitefly; the predatory mite *Phytoseiulus persimilis*, for red spider mite; the nematode *Steinernema kraussei*, for vine weevil; the ladybird beetle *Cryptolaemus montrouzieri*, used to control mealybugs.

For real success you need to catch the problem before the pest levels have built up, so get your biological controls in place as soon as you spot these fiends.

TIP Several specialist suppliers offer a mail-order service and will also give you telephone advice to help you tackle your specific problems.

Aubergines indoors

Aubergines fruit best in long, hot summers and love the extra warmth of being grown indoors.

Time to sow: early spring

Steady, warm temperatures and good humidity are the secrets to success with aubergines, which makes them perfect crops for a warm conservatory or greenhouse.

Sow seeds in trays, 8cm (3in) pots or modules at 15–21°C (59–70°F) and place in a propagator, warm greenhouse or on a windowsill. Pot on from trays or modules once the seedlings have three leaves, then grow on for a few weeks, potting on as necessary. Plant out into final-sized pots, 30cm (12in) in diameter, or plant two or three into grow bags.

Aim for a steady temperature of 15–18°C (59–65°F) and keep the compost moist but not waterlogged, misting the plants regularly with lukewarm water. Stake the plants with canes as they grow and feed every other watering with a half-strength tomato fertiliser.

Good varieties include 'Ova', which has small white fruits; 'Bambino' with dark, 'baby' fruits; 'Black Enorma', which produces a few huge, fat aubergines per plant.

TIP Soak the seeds overnight in warm water to improve germination.

Try biological pest controls

Aubergines indoors

Cloches extend the seasons

A simple cloche can help to extend the growing season – placing one over the soil early in the year warms the ground ready for planting.

Time to use: autumn–spring

Many plants and seeds simply will not grow if the soil is too cold, so a cloche convinces the plants that spring is on its way. It also offers valuable protection from chilly winds and rain, which can rapidly kill fragile young plants.

Use it in late winter for sowing early broad beans and at the end of the season to prolong the summer warmth for crops such as lettuces. Cloches are also useful for drying off harvested crops, such as onions and shallots, before they're stored.

You can make your own cloche using clear plastic, polythene or glass, or buy one ready made. The simplest cloche can be created with polythene stretched over a series of wire hoops and pegged down – it's also easy to put up and pack up in the shed when you don't need it.

Good varieties for growing under cloches include broad bean 'Aquadulce Claudia' and lettuce 'Marvel of Four Seasons'.

TIP Use the cloche hoops covered with netting as bird protection for brassicas in the summer months.

Windowsill propagator

A windowsill propagator gets the vegetable garden off to an early start and helps to keep crops coming all summer.

Time to sow: early spring

A compact propagator is one of the best ways to make the most of your kitchen windowsill – a seed tray with a plastic cover will do perfectly well, but you can also buy heated types.

Bottom heat is useful for germinating many seeds, and a plastic cover with adjustable air vents allows the humidity to be controlled to provide perfect growing conditions.

Long-term crops, such as chillies, peppers and aubergines, can be started off early in the season and kept at a constant temperature indoors. Quick growers, such as salads and herbs, can be germinated rapidly throughout the season and then potted on swiftly to make room to sow more seeds.

Good options include tomatoes, aubergines, peppers, and many salads and herbs.

TIP Use in summer to provide a quick crop of interesting mini leaves to add to salads, such as broccoli sprouts.

Windowsill propagator

Cloches extend the seasons

Grow winter lettuces

Keep the taste of summer coming over winter with home-grown lettuces.

Time to sow: late summer

Growing a handful of lettuces is great for those times when you feel like eating a winter salad but have none in the house. You can grow winter lettuces in grow bags or pots in a conservatory, greenhouse, or even in a large box on the kitchen windowsill.

Simply sow a few seeds in modules or pots in late summer and place in a bright spot until they germinate. Lettuces prefer cooler growing conditions, so make sure they are not in direct light. Thin out the weakest seedlings and leave the rest to grow on until they're large enough to transplant into pots or grow bags.

Lettuces can suffer from fungal diseases, so allow the air to get to them on warmer winter days by opening windows, vents or doors, or placing them outside for a couple of hours if they're in pots or a box.

Good varieties for growing indoors over winter include 'Winter Density' and 'Kwiek'.

TIP Start off seeds in winter and early spring to provide very early spring lettuces.

Herbs under a bell cloche

Growing plants under cover doesn't just mean greenhouses and conservatories – mini-cloches also provide good, portable protection.

Time to sow: early spring

Bell cloches act as miniature greenhouses for smaller plants such as herbs. Many annual herbs are fast growing but need warmth to get them up and running. Bought bell cloches, or ones made from large plastic drinks bottles with the bottom cut off, give young herbs that little bit of extra protection in cold temperatures.

All sorts of herbs can be started off in pots on a windowsill or in a propagator early in the season, then planted out under cloches from mid- to late spring. Do it this way and they should provide you with leaves for snipping within a few weeks – much quicker than those sown directly outside. To settle herbs in well as you plant them out, place cloches over the vacant soil where you want plants to grow a few weeks before planting to warm up the ground.

Good options include parsley, chervil and summer savory.

TIP Keep cropping parsley into winter by covering with a cloche in autumn.

Herbs under a bell cloche

Grow winter lettuces

Grow your own lemons

Turn your patio into a Mediterranean terrace with a fragrant lemon tree.

When to plant: spring–summer

A lemon tree makes a lovely feature plant on the patio in summer, with its fabulously scented flowers, glossy aromatic foliage and luscious ripening fruits.

These citrus plants are equally lovely in winter, too. Lemons and oranges should be moved into a greenhouse, conservatory or bright porch in autumn to protect them from frost. This warmth should also bring out the scent from the lemon flowers and foliage.

Lemons take little effort to grow in pots, as long as they're carefully watered and fed every month during the growing season. Citrus plants dislike lime, so when watering use rainwater or filtered water rather than straight from the tap.

Good varieties include 'Four Seasons', which has large fruits and can make a sizeable tree; 'Eureka', which is smaller but reliable and fruitful.

TIP Take care not to overwater or under water lemons – check the compost with your finger and aim to keep it evenly moist.

Growing peppers and chillies in pots

Spice up your menu with freshly picked peppers and chillies.

Time to sow: spring

Sweet peppers and chillies make great plants for growing in the greenhouse, conservatory or even on a sunny windowsill. Their attractive and colourful fruits can be added to curries, salsas and stir-fry dishes.

Sweet peppers need more room than chillies and will grow to 60–75cm (24–30in) high, depending on the variety. Some varieties of chilli reach only 15cm (6in) high, while others grow to 60cm (2ft).

Sow seeds in spring in a seed tray and place on a bright but not directly sunny windowsill, covered with a propagator or plastic bag until they germinate. Alternatively, buy ready-grown plug plants from the garden centre or nursery and pot on as necessary. The final pot size should be about 20–30cm (8–10in) in diameter, although it can be less for dwarf chillies.

Usually peppers and chillies branch well, but if they're a bit sparse looking, pinch out the tips when the plants are about 30cm (12in) high to encourage bushiness. Mist the plants regularly when they're in flower using lukewarm water to encourage the formation of fruits.

Good varieties include peppers 'Redskin' and 'Topepo Rosso'; chillies 'Anaheim' and 'Pyramid'.

TIP Chillies are more tolerant of fluctuating temperatures and haphazard watering than sweet peppers.

Wrap up your greenhouse for winter

If your greenhouse isn't heated, it's worth insulating it with bubble polythene to keep your plants as cosy as possible through the winter.

Time to do: all year round

Lining all the glass with a single layer of bubble polythene will mean fewer draughts, and if you do use a heater during the very coldest days, you won't need it on as often or for so long. Bubble polythene is readily available in garden centres, where it's sold by the metre. Choose UV-stabilised polythene that's specifically designed for greenhouses; this should last for at least three years if you look after it and store it properly. Before buying, measure the sides, roof and ends of your greenhouse so you know how much you need.

To cover the inside of your greenhouse, start with the sides, fixing the polythene to the frame using nails, drawing pins or wire, and pulling it taut for maximum insulation. When lining the roof, fix the polythene to the ridge and spread it down the glazing bars. Don't forget to cut and fasten the polythene around vents and louvres, so they can still be opened on warmer days.

TIP Choose polythene with large bubbles as this has better insulating properties and lets in more light.

Moving bananas under cover

Indoor cucumbers make interesting climbing plants in a conservatory or greenhouse.

Time to do: late autumn – early winter

Our recent mild winters might have lulled you into a false sense of security as far as tender plants are concerned, but don't let this winter be the one when the weather catches you out. If you live in a frost-prone area or your garden isn't very sheltered, and your tender exotics are small enough to be moved, bring them indoors before the weather turns cold.

Borderline hardy plants, such as the red banana, cannas and some palms, should be dug up and put in pots under cover over winter. If you're moving a canna or a banana, first cut off the lower leaves with a knife to make the plant easier to handle. Then dig around the plant with a spade and chop back some of the rootball to make it easier to pot up. Lift the plant using a fork, and brush most of the soil from the roots. Trim off any straggly roots with a knife, so they don't rot.

Transfer the plant into a small pot containing multi-purpose compost. Water well and stand in a frost-free place over winter.

TIP For advice on how to keep your soil warm through winter, turn to page 124.

Make your own mini-polytunnel

Don't waste money on expensive polytunnels – make your own.

Time to do: early spring

Start the season early with a home-made mini-polytunnel – it is ideal for bringing on early sowings of broad beans, peas and salads. You can easily move it around the garden to shelter new plantings, helping them get established and protecting them from cold and drying winds. It's just the thing to ripen off chillies and tomatoes, too, at the end of the season, as it's taller than most ready-made cloches.

An old, bendy tent frame makes the perfect support for a large sheet of polythene, which can be pegged into the ground using the tent pegs. You can buy UV-resistant polythene for a few pounds, and have it cut to the desired length, at most garden centres. This will last longer than ordinary polythene sheeting, especially if you roll it up and store it in the shed when not in use. The tent frame stores easily too – simply dismantle the poles and pop them back in their bag for next time.

TIP Keep both the ends open in summer for better ventilation.

Grow basil indoors

Get a genuine taste of Italy at home by growing your own basil.

Time to sow: spring

Basil is an essential herb for Italian cooking, and is an easy and rewarding plant to grow indoors, where it loves the warm temperatures and sheltered conditions.

In early or mid-spring, sow a few seeds in pots in a warm spot in a greenhouse, conservatory or on a windowsill. The temperature needs to be at least 16°C (60°F), otherwise they won't germinate – and even then they germinate slowly.

Once the seedlings are large enough, divide them up into individual pots or modules and grow them on. Pinch out the growing tips when they have a few leaves to encourage them to bush out.

Plant out into pots, window boxes or containers and harvest regularly to keep the plants producing more leaves. Before moving them outside, begin to acclimatise the young plants in early summer by putting them outdoors for a few hours at a time during the day, bringing them back in at night.

Good varieties include 'Sweet Genovese', with classic, large, fragrant green leaves; 'Purple Ruffles', which has very dark, purple-black leaves and a delicious flavour.

TIP Don't be tempted to move plants outside before early summer, as basil is very tender.

Make your own mini-polytunnel

Grow basil indoors

Sowing seeds

Get crops off to an early start by sowing seeds indoors.

Time to sow: spring–early summer

Make the most of your warm windowsills, spare room or conservatory to get some seeds sown before the final frosts are over.

Many seeds take several weeks to germinate and grow before they're large enough to plant out. Getting a few things started in a warm spot indoors means plants will be ready to go into the ground as soon as the weather turns milder.

Make the most of your space by sowing into cells or modules, as they don't take up as much room as pots, but do give the germinating seedlings enough root room to grow on for a few weeks before they need potting on or planting out.

Fill the modules with compost and tap firmly to settle it down. Try to sow only one or two seeds per module to save you thinning them out later. Start off salads and herbs such as parsley in this way, then when they're large enough to plant out, harden them off by putting them outside for a few hours at a time. Once they are acclimatised to the outdoors, plant them straight out into the garden under fleece or cloches.

Good options include lettuces, herbs, peppers, tomatoes and chillies.

TIP Label each set of modules clearly, otherwise you could get very confused once they all start coming up.

Force mint in winter

You can have fresh mint at your fingertips even in winter. Plant just a few roots and you can have mint sauce whenever you want it.

Time to plant: early autumn

Mint is such a strong grower that it's easy and fun to force it for the winter months. Dig up a few roots from plants growing out in the garden in early autumn and plant them in a container filled with multi-purpose compost. Lay the roots down lengthways on the soil surface and lightly cover with compost. Water and place in a greenhouse, conservatory or on a bright windowsill.

Keep the compost slightly damp, but be careful not to overwater – check by pushing your finger into the compost. New shoots should start to appear within a couple of weeks. Pot them up and keep them indoors on a sunny windowsill. Cut leaves regularly throughout the winter and the plant will grow bushier and will keep going until spring.

TIP Use an old olive-oil tin or an attractive wine box lined with polythene as a container if you want to grow mint on the kitchen windowsill.

Force mint in winter

Sowing seeds

Make your own comfrey feed, page 183

Top tips for making the most of your crops

Sow peas in loo-roll tubes

Economise with space and money by sowing pea and bean plants in toilet-roll middles.

Time to sow: spring

The cardboard middles of toilet rolls make perfect biodegradable pots for deep-rooting legumes. Peas and beans are large and fast-growing plants, and they need plenty of root room to develop properly. They also hate cold soil and can germinate very patchily if sown directly into the ground early in the season.

Start early peas off indoors in early spring, and save money and space by using toilet-roll tubes instead of traditional plastic pots, which are wider and not as deep. Fill each tube with compost and plant one or two peas about 2.5cm (1in) deep.

Grow on until large enough to plant out, then harden off by putting the plants outside on warmer days, bringing them back in at night. Plant out without removing their tubes, as these will quickly rot away in the soil. Use twiggy sticks or netting to support the plants as they grow.

Good varieties include pea 'Feltham First', which is an early variety; 'Sugar Snap', which produces sweet pods that can be left to form peas.

TIP In mild areas, sow peas outdoors in autumn to overwinter for next season. Protect with cloches if the weather turns bitterly cold.

Mulch to conserve moisture

Cut down on weeds and reduce the need for watering by mulching.

Time to do: summer

Fast-growing plants need plenty of water during warm weather to keep them growing and producing crops. Adding a thick layer of mulch after watering or rainfall helps to stop the water evaporating from the soil surface in the heat of the sun, and keeps the moisture close to the roots, where it is needed.

Simply add a thick 5cm (2in) layer of garden compost, well-rotted manure or bark chippings around the base of plants such as tomatoes, courgettes and beans on a regular basis. Lay it on the soil surface and do not dig it in.

TIP Mulching helps to cut down on emerging weeds by smothering them and covering the seeds so they don't have enough light to germinate.

Sow peas in loo-roll tubes

Mulch to conserve moisture

Good housekeeping

Help reduce the risk of pest and disease attack by making tidying up part of your weekly routine.

Time to do: all year round

Routine inspections and a few key jobs take no time at all and can make the world of difference to your crops. Healthy, happy plants will produce a more bountiful harvest, so keep an eye open for disease and remove affected plants swiftly to stop infections spreading. Burn any infected plants or put them in the bin, not on the compost heap.

Try to do little things regularly, such as trimming off yellowing, fading leaves from brassicas to reduce the risk of disease and so that slugs and snails have fewer places to hide. A quick weeding session reduces competition for water and lets rain get to the soil and plants more easily.

Cushioning developing strawberries with straw lifts them off the soil and lessens the chance of them rotting. It also retains moisture in the soil, which is vital for the developing fruit. A thick mulch of scratchy straw also helps to keep slugs at bay (see p78).

TIP Pick off pests such as cabbage white caterpillars and blackfly by hand before they get a hold.

Winter-prune apple trees

Prune apples and pears in winter to get the best shape.

Time to do: winter

The winter months offer the ideal opportunity to get apple and pear trees looking good and growing well.

After leaf fall in autumn, the trees are dormant and pruning cuts have time to heal well before the trees burst back into life in spring. Also, without leaves you can see the shape of the tree more clearly, which makes it easier to decide which branches to prune.

Always remove any dead, diseased or badly damaged branches first, and then try to create an open shape, removing any weak or spindly growth to encourage other branches to thicken up.

Keep a mixture of older stems and new growth, because if you cut back too hard you could have little or no fruit the following year. Cut branches back to the junction with another large branch, or even the trunk, rather than just trimming off lots of spindly branches, to ensure a good fruit crop the next year.

TIP Cut back the tallest leading shoot every year to keep the tree at the size you want.

Winter-prune apple trees

Good housekeeping

Make a string of chillies

Brighten up your food and kitchen with this cheery way of storing chillies.

Time to do: autumn

Store chillies in the traditional way by threading them on a string. This is how they do it in Spain and Mexico – freshly picked chillies are hung up to dry to strengthen their flavour and boost their heat.

Strings of chillies look great in the kitchen and make lovely Christmas presents too. Harvest chillies in late summer and autumn by cutting them from the plant, leaving a long stalk on each fruit. Use red or green string for a seasonal look, and tie the chillies on in small bunches of four or five in several clusters up the string. Add a parcel label with the variety name on it, if you like, and leave a long piece of string at the top to make a loop for hanging it up.

TIP Chillies contain a strong irritant, so wash your hands thoroughly after handling them and don't rub your eyes.

Storing onions and garlic

Plaited into strings, onions and garlic keep for months and are easy and space-saving to store.

Time to do: late summer

Garlic and onions are must-haves for cooking, and if stored in plaited strings they're always on hand for use.

Onions and garlic must be really ripe and dry to store well, especially if you make them into strings like this. If one bulb rots, it will infect the bulbs next to it and the whole string could be ruined – so keep checking the bulbs to make sure none is deteriorating.

Once you've harvested your onions, lay them on the ground under cloches or put them in the greenhouse or conservatory to dry off thoroughly. The skins should become papery and dry to the touch. Then simply bunch together the onions to form an attractive string or weave the strong, rope-like tops together to make a plait.

TIP Onions also store well in old nylon tights, but these don't look as good hanging in the kitchen!

Make a string of chillies

Storing onions and garlic

Apples for keeps

With a little careful preparation, you can be eating apples long after harvest time.

Time to do: autumn

You can store many varieties of cooking and eating apples through the winter. Even a small apple tree can produce a surprising quantity of fruit.

Apples are prolific fruiters, especially 'Bramley's Seedling' and other cooking varieties. It's worth storing some to see you through the winter months. Only store the best-quality fruit – eat those with any bruises or blemishes straight away.

Check the fruit carefully first, then wrap in newspaper or put them in plastic bags pierced with several holes and store in boxes or trays in a cool, dark place, such as a garage.

Unwrap and check the fruit regularly for any signs of rot or softness. Remove and use any that show signs of deteriorating.

TIP Store wrapped apples in boxes, crates or even filing trays.

Storing potatoes in sacks

Make your harvest last all winter.

Time to do: late summer

Dig up maincrop potatoes in late summer and you can store them to keep you going over winter. Most maincrop-potato varieties store exceptionally well over several months simply kept in brown paper or hessian sacks.

Dry the harvested potatoes off by laying them out on newspaper in a shed, conservatory, greenhouse, or even the spare room. Cover them with more paper or an old curtain and allow them to dry off for a week or two before carefully placing them in the sacks. Make sure they are not bruised or damaged, and that there are no signs of rot or slug holes. Put any damaged ones aside and eat them quickly.

Store the sacks of potatoes in a cool, but not cold, place – a garage is ideal – and check regularly for any signs of rot. Keep them in the dark to prevent them from sprouting.

Early and second-early potatoes cannot be stored in this way. They keep well in the fridge or a cool shed or a garage, but only for about a week. So if you grow these, harvest them only as and when you need them.

TIP Store different varieties in different sacks so you can do a taste and storage test.

Apples for keeps

Storing potatoes in sacks

Cropping to encourage more

The more you pick, the more plants produce.

Time to do: summer

Harvesting regularly throughout the season keeps plants producing more leaves, beans, pods and fruits.

Crops that aren't harvested quickly often stop producing, as the plants form seeds and complete their life cycle. Regular picking of crops makes them produce more and keeps them small and flavoursome, rather than big, old and tasteless.

Beans and peas need to be picked as soon as they're large enough, even if you only get a handful, otherwise the pods soon swell and turn stringy as the seeds ripen inside. The plants will then produce no more flowers and the pods stop forming.

Harvest courgettes every other day once the plant is in full swing, as a small courgette will swell into a huge marrow in no time at all. Salad leaves, such as cut-and-come-again varieties, rocket and chard, should be picked every week. Either cut them to 5cm (2in) above the ground or simply pluck off the outer leaves, leaving the centre to produce more.

TIP Try to pick a little every day if you can, as crops develop swiftly during the summer months.

Planting in containers

Container gardening is perfect if you're short on space – it is practical and fun on a balcony or in a tiny garden.

Time to plant: spring–summer

Most crops will grow well in containers, providing the pot is large enough to allow the plants' roots to develop fully. As a general rule, the larger the pot, the better the plants will grow, and this is especially true of long-term plants such as fruit bushes and trees. Short-term crops can be grown in smaller pots and boxes, though, as they don't have time to develop extensive root systems.

When transplanting pot- or module-grown plants, always replant at the same level. Place some broken-up polystyrene or old pots in the bottom for drainage, then part-fill the new pot with compost. Make a hole in the compost for the plant, then settle it in gently, trying not to damage any fragile roots. Top up with compost to the level at which it was planted before, and firm the plant in with your hands. Don't bury the stem of the plant beneath the compost, as this could cause rot to set in. Don't leave the roots above the compost either, as the plant could dry out.

TIP Water newly potted plants well to settle the compost around their roots.

Cropping to encourage more

Planting in containers

Sow green manure

After your crops are harvested, rather than forking in well-rotted manure or compost, grow a green manure. It enriches and breaks up the soil, needing only a minimal amount of digging.

Time to do: all year round

Green manures are plants sown directly into bare ground purely to be dug back into the soil in order to improve its fertility and boost the organic content. They also keep weeds at bay on an empty plot by covering the soil so they can't grow.

You can leave green manures in place for anything up to a year if you wish, but most gardeners don't have the luxury of that much space. It's usually best to opt for a crop that is sown and grown in just six weeks. If you need a quick fix in summer, sow buckwheat, mustard, phacelia or fenugreek; in the winter months grow winter tares or Italian ryegrass (though this needs a little more digging in than other green manures).

It's important not to let the plants flower, and if they look like they're about to, simply chop off the tops. When you're ready to use the bed again, cut the plants down to the ground, leave for a day or two, then dig them back into the soil.

TIP If you do have an area of ground that you won't be cultivating for a year, then sow a long-term manure, such as winter beans, red clover or alfalfa. Chop the plants back occasionally to keep them under control until you're ready to dig them in.

Keep sowing herbs

Regular small sowings will keep you in fresh, young herbs all summer long.

Time to sow: spring–summer

Growing a handful of culinary herbs in the garden, in pots or in window boxes, can transform a range of cooked dishes and salads with no effort at all. Just a sprig or two of freshly-picked herbs will add oodles of flavour to any recipe.

Many perennials, such as thyme and rosemary, can be cropped year after year, but some of the top culinary herbs are annuals and need to be sown fresh each year. These include coriander, basil, chervil and dill, but all these are also prone to producing flowers, setting seed and fading very quickly, well before the season has finished. So, ideally, you should make about three or four repeat sowings, about 3 weeks apart, to keep the fresh young leaves coming.

Sow seeds thinly on the surface of moist compost from spring onwards, cover with a thin layer of compost and put the pots on a warm windowsill. As the seedlings appear, re-pot the herbs into bigger pots and move them outside. Start picking leaves as soon as they are big enough for cropping.

TIP Dill and coriander readily run to seed, but the seeds are actually very tasty, so save those from the fading plants while harvesting leaves from the new sowings.

Keep sowing herbs

Grow green manure

Parsnips for winter eating

Parsnips are a long-term crop with lots of flavour, so make them part of your crop rotation to harvest as you need them over winter.

Time to sow: mid-spring

Growing parsnips does take time, as they're sown in spring and ideally not harvested until after the first frosts, so they're as sweet as possible. However, you can dig them up earlier than that, especially if you prefer them as baby vegetables. Although parsnips take up room in the garden for a long period of time, they're a reliable and worthwhile crop to grow.

Sow the fine, papery seeds in drills on a still day, as they tend to blow away easily. Parsnips like finely textured soil that they can send roots through easily, so good soil preparation is essential. Avoid recently manured or stony soil, as this makes the roots fork. Sow seeds thinly, around 2.5cm (1in) apart, in rows 30cm (12in) apart, then thin the seedlings to 15cm (6in) apart once they appear. Do not transplant seedlings.

Good varieties include 'Avonresister', which is resistant to canker and good on poor soils; 'Tender and True', a classic variety.

TIP As parsnips are slow to germinate and grow, you can sow fast-maturing crops such as lettuces and radishes alongside to make the most of the space in spring.

Grow a quick crop of pak choi

Leafy and nutritious pak choi takes hardly any time to grow. Pop a few plants into odd spaces as you harvest other crops.

Time to sow: spring–summer

Pak choi is a delicious baby vegetable that can be eaten whole, braised or steamed, or the leaves tossed in stir-fries. Although an oriental leaf vegetable, it grows easily and so swiftly here that it's the perfect 'filler' crop. You can treat it as a cut-and-come-again and start harvesting baby leaves for salads after only about 2 weeks, or you can leave the plants to grow to full size within a couple of months. Don't let them grow for too long, though, or they will bolt and will become unappetising.

Choose F1 hybrids, as these are more resistant to bolting, and sow into modules in mid-spring, planting out good-sized plants once the frosts have passed. Harvest mature plants before the chilly days begin, as pak choi tends to bolt if the weather is too cold. Protect developing plants from pigeons with netting.

Good varieties include 'Joi Choi', which has some resistance to bolting; 'Red Choi', which is nice in salads.

TIP Water plentifully during the growing season for good crops.

Parsnips for winter eating

Grow a quick crop of pak choi

Recycling ideas

Be kind to your purse and the environment and grow seedlings in containers made from household waste.

Time to do: all year round

With a little ingenuity and time you can re-use a number of things that would otherwise end up in the bin.

Washed-out margarine tubs, yogurt cartons and milk containers make marvellous pots for growing seedlings, if you punch a few drainage holes through the bottom.

Cardboard cartons and toilet-roll tubes are brilliant for growing deep-rooted beans or sweet peas (see p166). There's no need to remove them when planting, either, as they'll quickly rot away in the soil. Egg boxes can be used like small peat pots for growing lettuces and herbs, and will also rot in the ground. Re-use white plastic bottles or margarine tubs by cutting them into pieces to make labels, and save foil trays, free CDs and tin foil to make bird scarers by tying them together with string.

TIP Small yogurt-drink pots make excellent cane toppers to protect your eyes and stop protective netting becoming holed.

Plant bare-root trees and shrubs

Winter brings a slowdown for plants and gardeners, making it the perfect time to plant bare-rooted trees and shrubs.

Time to plant: winter

Bare-root trees and shrubs are a cheap way of buying plants, and are available for sale from nurseries and mail-order companies in winter. This is the best time to plant these trees and shrubs, as they settle in and establish more successfully if they're planted after leaf fall, when they're dormant.

Take time to prepare the planting site in advance, and ideally plant your trees or shrubs as soon after you receive them as possible in order to get them off to a good start. The roots may need trimming first to remove any that are dead, damaged or excessively long. (See p69 for how to plant.)

TIP If staking your tree, position the stake alongside the tree before filling the planting hole with soil again.

Watering wisely

Vegetables and fruit rely on a plentiful supply of water to keep them growing.

Time to do: spring–summer, mainly

Watering wisely and at the right time is essential for producing healthy, abundant crops. Plants are mostly made up of water and the soil acts as a reservoir for their roots.

Digging organic matter into the soil improves its water-holding capacity, and adding a thick layer of mulch to the soil surface helps to stop moisture evaporating. But when there's no rainfall, sometimes watering is essential. Try to save as much water as possible in water butts, and remove weeds regularly so they don't take up valuable moisture.

When you do need to water, give each plant or row of plants a thorough drink – don't just sprinkle the surface with water. Leaf and root crops need regular watering at all stages, whereas fruiting crops such as tomatoes and beans critically need watering when they're just planted, when they're in flower, and once the fruit begins to swell.

TIP Water in the early evening to allow the soil and plants to soak up the moisture, and to reduce water loss by evaporation from the sun.

Make your own comfrey feed

This organic liquid fertiliser is simple to make, and you can use it to feed all your crops.

Time to do: late spring–summer

Comfrey liquid feed is a marvellous all-round fertiliser that can be made cheaply and conveniently from home-grown plants. Although liquid feeds like this one don't last long in the soil, they do give plants a valuable boost in summer when growth is at its strongest.

Comfrey (*Symphytum* spp.) is a low-maintenance, ground-covering perennial that will romp its way through poor soils and can become rather invasive if not kept in check. This makes it perfect for hard cropping and putting on the compost heap, or using as a liquid feed.

To make liquid comfrey feed, gather handfuls of comfrey leaves and place them in a hessian or net bag, then steep in a water butt or large bucket of water for a couple of weeks. The resulting liquid is dark, oily and very smelly, but full of potassium. It can be diluted in a watering can to feed your crops at a rate of one part comfrey liquid to ten parts water.

TIP If you don't have access to any comfrey, use nettles to make a feed that is equally nutritious and beneficial.

Common pests – vine weevils

These little white larvae can make a real meal of your crops in pots.

Time to do: spring–summer

Vine weevil larvae can be a problem if you grow lots of crops in pots; they will live in the compost and eat the roots of plants and seedlings.

Vine weevils love to lay their eggs in containers of compost, and their larvae can destroy crops from the bottom up, eating away the entire root system of a plant. So check the compost for these distinctive white, legless grubs with a brown head.

Luckily these pests are very easy to control with biological nematodes, which can be watered on to the compost and last for several weeks. The treatment is expensive, but if you grow a lot of things in pots then a couple of applications during the summer months are well worthwhile.

The adult weevils – dull black beetles – are relatively easy to spot as they're very slow moving and have distinctive bent or 'elbowed' antennae. They are mainly nocturnal and tend to hide in dark corners during the day, so keep an eye open for them at dusk.

TIP A good way to catch the adults is to place toilet-roll tubes or small pots filled with straw in pots and containers. Check the traps regularly and destroy any adults you find.

Timely protection

Be sure to get good crops by protecting your outdoor plants.

Time to do: Winter, spring and early summer, depending on the crop

A little protection at the crucial time can make all the difference. Pests and late frosts can spoil your chances of a good harvest. Birds are particularly troublesome when it comes to fruit bushes, but a drape of fine-mesh netting pegged down or weighted with large stones will prevent them getting to the fruit before you. However, do bear in mind that wildlife and birds can get trapped in netting, so check it daily to ensure that no wildlife is harmed.

It's best to raise and support the netting with canes if you can, as this stops the foliage growing through and making the netting difficult to remove without damaging the plant.

Pigeons are especially fond of brassicas and can reduce them to a skeleton of leaf ribs virtually overnight. Again, a frame of canes covered with netting over the brassicas will help. Do this when they're planted out and leave in place until harvest time.

Fruit-tree blossom, especially on trained specimens, is very susceptible to late frosts, which can ruin your chances of a good crop. If frost is forecast, protect delicate blossom with fleece or polythene pinned over the plant, and again secure it with large stones at the base .

TIP If you haven't got large stones, use tent pegs or U-shaped pieces of wire to secure netting into the ground.

Common pests – vine weevils

Timely protection

Common pests – whitefly

These small but destructive pests often appear on plants in large numbers in greenhouses and conservatories.

Time to do: spring–summer

Whitefly suck the sap of plants such as tomatoes and cucumbers, often hiding on the underside of their foliage. They also attack young plants and seedlings, as well as houseplants.

These pests are difficult to eradicate once they become established, so check plants regularly and take action as soon as you spot any. They weaken plants and disfigure them with spots on the leaves, sticky honeydew and sooty moulds.

In the greenhouse, a biological control such as the tiny parasitic wasp *Encarsia formosa* can be used – a good garden centre will have details of suppliers, or search online. Alternatively, hang yellow sticky cards above plants in the greenhouse to trap them. In the house, use a small hand-held vacuum cleaner to suck them off the plants.

Sprays are available for whitefly control. Follow the directions carefully as these only kill whitefly and not their eggs. Regular spraying is required to kill newly emerged adults before they lay more eggs.

TIP The yellow traps catch whitefly that fly up when disturbed. So brush the foliage of infected plants with your hands to get the pests moving.

Common pests – blackfly

A familiar sight to many, these clusters of black aphids can quickly cover a plant.

Time to take action: early–mid-summer

Dense clusters of blackfly can spread rapidly, sucking the sap and weakening the plant enough to ruin the crop.

The good thing about these tiny pests is that they are very easy to spot. They appear in late spring and early summer, clustering on the soft tips of plants and on the developing bean pods of broad beans in particular. They're also common on many flowering plants, especially nasturtiums, and once they get a hold they're hard to get rid of completely.

Act early by pinching off the growing shoots of broad beans and nasturtiums, and squirt off small clusters with a jet of water or squash them by hand. If the problem is severe, organic sprays are also available.

TIP Encourage natural predators into your garden, such as blue tits and ladybirds, by putting up bird and bug boxes.

Common pests – blackfly

Common pests – whitefly

Common pests – carrot root fly

Protect your carrot crop from these menaces in the summer months.

Time to do: early summer

Simple protection methods will keep your carrots free of carrot root fly. These pests lay their eggs in the soil near carrots, and the larvae munch their way through the core of carrots from early summer until autumn, destroying the crop.

Sowing seeds thinly helps prevent the problem, as the adult flies are attracted to the smell of carrots when you're thinning the crop. They're also low flying, so a simple barrier only 30cm (12in) high all the way around the carrot bed will protect them. Use canes and fleece or polythene secured with string or wire. Alternatively, cover the entire crop with a thin-gauge fleece or a densely woven mesh so the light can still get to the crop.

If you have space, grow onions or chives around your carrots, as the smell from these will help disguise that of the carrots and should deter the flies.

Good carrot varieties include 'Flyaway' and 'Sytan' – both of which appear to be less attractive to the pest.

TIP Delay harvesting carrots until autumn to avoid attracting the adult flies.

Common pests – slugs and snails

The bane of every gardener's life ...

Time to do: spring

Slugs and snails love seedlings and tender young crops. Slugs decimate ground-level crops and emerging seedlings, while snails are also energetic climbers and will readily find their way into containers and pots.

It is when plants are small and succulent that they are particularly vulnerable to slugs and snails. Once plants have reached a good size and are growing strongly and fruiting consistently, they can usually survive all but the worst slug attacks.

The best ways to deal with these unwelcome visitors are either to use organically approved slug pellets little and often around crops, or to go on regular slug and snail hunts at dusk, disposing of them by whatever method you prefer. Some gardeners chop them up, drown them, or transport them some distance away. Beer traps are another popular choice, but do remember to empty them regularly. Copper rings or tape around pot rims are also very effective, giving snails a tiny electric shock when they pass over them.

TIP Use barriers such as grit, broken egg shells or manufactured slug gels and barriers to prevent slugs and snails getting to your crops.

Common pests – carrot root fly

Common pests – slugs and snails

Index

Picture credits

BBC Books and Gardeners' World Magazine would like to thank the following for providing photographs. While every effort has been made to trace and acknowledge all photographers, we would like to apologise should there be any errors or omissions.

11t Jason Ingram (design: Jekka McVicar/Lisa Buckland), 11b Freia Turland/Dig Pictures, 13t David Murray, 13b Noel Murphy; 15t Ben Murphy, 15b Jason Ingram; 17t Torie Chugg (design: Paul Williams); 17b Jason Ingram; 21t Lynn Keddie, 21b Stephen Hamilton; 23t Jason Ingram, 23b Stephen Hamilton; 25t Mark Bolton, 25b Jason Ingram; 27t Ben Murphy, 27b Paul Debois (design: Cinean McTernan); 31t Freia Turland/Dig Pictures, 31b Tim Sandall; 33t Jason Ingram (design: GW Live, Garden of Three R's); 33b Jason Ingram (design: GW Live, The Good Life with Bradstone); 37t and 37b Jason Ingram; 39t Tim Sandall, 39b Jason Ingram; 43t and 43b Tim Sandall, 45t Mark Bolton (design: Bob Purnell); 45b William Shaw; 47t Jason Ingram, 47b Peter Anderson; 51t Tim Sandall, 51b Nick Smith; 53t Caroline Hughes, 53b Tim Sandall; 55t Jason Ingram (design: Summer Solstice Garden, Chelsea Flower Show 2008: del Buono Gazerwitz, Spencer Fung Architects), 55b, 59t Sarah Cuttle; 59b, 61t Stephen Hamilton, 61b Torie Chugg; 65t Anne Hyde, 65b Sarah Heneghan; 67t, 67b Tim Sandall; 71t Jason Ingram, 71b Sarah Heneghan; 73t Stephen Hamilton, 73b Sarah Heneghan; 77t, 77b, 79t Stephen Hamilton; 79b Noel Murphy; 80 Mike Harding; 83t Paul Debois, 83b Jason Ingram; 85t Jason Ingram, 85b Stephen Hamilton; 89t Jason Ingram (design: Jekka McVicar/Lisa Buckland), 89b Stephen Hamilton; 91t Sarah Heneghan, 91b Lynn Keddie; 95b Sarah Heneghan; 97t Jason Ingram; 98 Stephen Hamilton; 101t, 101b Tim Sandall; 103t Melanie Eclare, 103b Sarah Cuttle; 107t Tim Sandall, 107b Stephen Marwood; 109t, 109b Sarah Heneghan; 113t Caroline Hughes, 113b Stephen Hamilton; 117t Sarah Heneghan, 117b Tim Sandall; 119t Stephen Hamilton; 121t William Shaw, 121b Stephen Hamilton; 123t Tim Sandall, 123b Noel Murphy; 127t Tim Sandall, 127b Sarah Heneghan; 131b Stephen Hamilton; 135t William Shaw, 135b Sarah Heneghan; 137t Tim Sandall, 137b Sarah Heneghan; 139t, 139b Stephen Hamilton; 141t Tim Sandall, 141b Nick Smith; 142 Gardeners' World Magazine; 145t William Shaw, 145b Tim Sandall; 147t Tim Sandall, 147b Stephen Hamilton; 149t Tim Sandall, 149b Simon Wheeler; 153t William Shaw, 153b Tim Sandall; 155t Michelle Garratt, 155b Sarah Cuttle; 157t Gavin Kingcome, 157b Stephen Hamilton; 161t Nick Smith, 161b Tim Sandall; 163t Paul Debois, 163b Caroline Hughes; 164 Nick Smith; 167t Tim Sandall, 167b Caroline Hughes; 169t Tim Sandall, 169b Jason Ingram (Toby Buckland); 171t, 171b Jason Ingram; 173t Paul Debois, 174t Nick Smith; 177t, 177b Stephen Hamilton; 179t Caroline Hughes, 179b Tim Sandall; 181t, 181b Jason Ingram; 185t Tim Sandall, 185b Nick Smith; 187t Paul Debois, 187b Tim Sandall.